The Skills of Teaching:

Content Development Skills

David H. Berenson, Ph.D.
Sally R. Berenson, M.S. Ed.
Robert R. Carkhuff, Ph.D.

CARKHUFF
INSTITUTE
of HUMAN
TECHNOLOGY

Human
Resource
Development
Press

Publishers of Human Technology

D1456106

 *Human Resource Development Press* Box 863, Dept. M61, Amherst, Massachusetts 01002

Publishers of Human Technology   1-413-253-3488

International Standard Book Number: 0-914234-21-8
Library of Congress Number: 77-091639
First Printing: March, 1978

Designed and Illustrated by Tom Capolongo
Consulting Editor, David V. Rowland

TABLE
OF
CONTENTS

The Skills of Teaching: Content Development Skills

ABOUT THE AUTHORS

Dr. David H. Berenson is Director of Educational Technology, Carkhuff Institute of Human Technology. He specializes in teacher training and educational administration. A teacher for more than 15 years on elementary and secondary grade levels, Dr. Berenson has spent the last 10 years revolutionizing pre-service and in-service teacher training programs, in addition to conducting pathfinding research in the development of effective educational delivery systems. Dr. Berenson is co-author of the entire **Skills of Teaching** series.

Sally R. Berenson, M.S. Ed., is Research Associate in Educational Technology, Carkhuff Institute of Human Technology, and has specialized in curriculum development. Mrs. Berenson has been an elementary and secondary teacher for more than ten years. She has instructed teachers at all levels of pre-service and in-service teacher training, and is a collaborator on the series **The Do's and Don'ts of Teaching**.

Dr. Robert R. Carkhuff is Chairman, Carkhuff Institute of Human Technology, and has devoted his life to research and teaching. The author of more than two dozen books on helping and teaching effectiveness, Dr. Carkhuff is internationally renowned as the most-cited reference in the last decade of counseling psychology. A teacher at primary, secondary, and post-secondary levels, he continues to coach youth baseball, basketball, and football. Dr. Carkhuff is developer of the human and educational resource development models upon which **The Skills of Teaching** series is based.

The Authors and Their Teachers

FOREWORD

In the forefront of the effort to build a human technology are the authors of **The Skills of Teaching** series. With more than a decade of research concerning teaching and helping processes and outcomes, Dr. Carkhuff and his colleagues have developed the necessary skills teaching programs that create a human technology for human effectiveness — skills teaching programs that will enable children and parents, as well as teachers, to achieve and enjoy success in learning.

In this volume, the authors address the personalized **content development skills** which enable the teachers to develop their specialty content into a skills objective. They derive this skills objective from the yearly content, and specify the **think** and **do** steps needed to develop the daily content, developing the levels of supportive **facts, concepts,** and **principles** needed to support the acquisition of skills.

The appearance of **The Skills of Teaching** series represents a landmark in educational technology. These skills programs were developed by and in conjunction with classroom teachers — those in the front lines of education.

The Skills of Teaching series teaches the kind of concrete skills a veteran teacher might wish to have had at the start of a teaching career. This is the kind of teacher training curriculum that an outstanding teacher-educator might develop over several decades, an accomplishment of human technology.

The Skills of Teaching series enables teachers to master teaching skills and, at the same time, to begin to measure the progress of their learners. In time, the learners are able to measure their own progress, and help to control the learning process.

With careful study and planning, teachers and parents soon discover that they are the source of their children's effectiveness. The outcome of this planning is symmetry and harmony. People become truly human beings — because they recognize that all of their children are exceptional.

January 1978
Washington, D. C.

James W. Becker, Ed. D.
Executive Director
National Foundation for the
Improvement of Education

In the **National Consortium for Humanizing Education**, we taught **The Skills of Teaching** to hundreds of elementary and secondary teachers all over the country, studying the effects of our teacher training upon over 6,000 students.

What we found, was that the learners of teachers with the skills of teaching demonstrated significantly greater growth and development than those whose teachers had not. Most importantly, teachers could be systematically trained to develop their teaching skills.

The trained teachers were most effective in maintaining **control** and reducing **dicipline** problems in the classroom, and also in facilitating student achievement in **basic skills**.

In **The Skills of Teaching — Content Development Skills**, the Carkhuff Model picks up with its principles, objectives, and programs where others leave off with facts and concepts. The authors define the skills in terms that are observable and measurable, and do so from the teacher's frame of reference. Most importantly, they deliver a product — developed content personalized for learners.

The Skills of Teaching is the most revolutionary step forward in the history of education. Together, the volumes constitute the teacher's answer to accountability: **the preservation of the integrity of teaching, and production of measurable outcome through increasing the quantity and quality of teaching skills.**

We owe a great debt of gratitude to Dr. Carkhuff, Dr. and Mrs. Berenson, and their associates for making possible the second greatest privilege in the world — effective teaching.

January, 1978

David N. Aspy, Ed. D.
Executive Director
National Consortium for
Humanizing Education

This volume of **The Skills of Teaching** focuses upon **Content Development Skills**. Before the teacher sets foot in the classroom, a content must be developed. The teacher must organize the yearly content, and then develop the skills and supportive knowledge that must be taught in the daily content. These content development skills emphasize the personalized content dimensions of teaching.

Facts are the names or labels which help the learners to identify something.

Concepts are the meanings which we attach to things that tell the learners what things do.

Principles are the relationships between facts and concepts, which tell the learners why things do what they do.

Skills are the observable and measurable things that learners must do.

Skill Steps are the steps that learners must perform to achieve the skills objective.

These content development skills will prepare you to develop your individual content into a skills objective. Used in conjunction with your interpersonal and teaching delivery skills, these content development skills are the basic tools of teaching effectiveness, and your entry into the exciting world of teaching.

January, 1978   D.H.B.
Amherst, Massachusetts   S.R.B.
                                                 R.R.C.

SECTION I. ORGANIZING YOUR YEARLY CONTENT

Shafted!

September.

"We got shafted!" Tim's stone struck the STOP sign squarely in the middle, and the metallic **clang** underscored his irritation.

"Yeah, we sure did . . ." Marty scuffed his sneakers along the sidewalk, doing his best to wear away their offensive newness. It just wasn't fair! He and Tim had always been in the same classroom. Well, always for the last two years, anyway, and now some jerk had made a mistake and put them in two different 4th grade classes. Heck, the classrooms weren't even near each other! The whole thing stunk, it really did.

"What's your teacher like?" Tim wanted to know.

"Mr. Huston?" Marty scowled, remembering his new teacher's roving gaze and his stern, no-nonsense voice. "Huh — he thinks he's in the army or something! All he kept sayin' was how we were gonna do everything by the book, no messin' around, really gonna get down to the basics . . ."

"What's that mean?"

Marty shrugged. He couldn't care less. "How'm I s'posed to know? He just kept yellin' about 'the basics' all day long." He pushed a hank of brown hair out of his eyes. "What's your teacher like?"

Tim grinned. "Her name's Miz Principato. She seems like she might be kinda neat — like she's gonna let us do whatever we want this year. She thinks it's real important for kids to get excited 'bout learning and stuff like that."

Marty scowled again at the unfairness of it all. "Yeah? She must be whacko or something." Then his gaze lifted and his face relaxed into a broad grin as, excitedly, he punched Tim on the arm. "Hey, look — there's old Missie's brother with his motorcycle! C'mon, maybe he'll give us a ride!" School forgotten, the two friends raced down the street together.

January.

Tim pressed his nose against the cold glass, trying to feel the impact of the sleet bombarding the world outside of the window. Four floors below, a chilled and windy greyness assaulted the few people foolish enough to be out on this early Sunday evening. The weather seemed a perfect reflection of Tim's mood.

"Boy, I sure wish we didn't have to go back to school tomorrow."

Across the living room of Tim's parents' apartment, Marty sat with his nose in a comic book, caught up in the latest exploits of the Amazing Spider Man. "Me too," Marty agreed without looking up. Then something about Tim's statement pricked his curiosity. "Hey, I thought you said Miz Principato was so neat. Wasn't she letting you all work on some kind of ecol - ecol - -"

"Ecology project." Tim supplied the phrase without turning from the window. "Yeah, she's still letting us do that — or anything else we want to do — but it really gets boring! I mean, she just gives us all this stuff and then stands around grinning and expecting us to do somethin' with it. It's really dumb!"

"Yeah?" Marty sounded skeptical. "I don't know . . . I wish we got to do stuff like that. All Mr. Huston does is go over and over the same stupid things. Like this week, we were supposed to learn about adding numbers." He snorted with disgust. "Heck, I learned that junk years ago! But he keeps sayin' it's all part of the basics. We spent every math class adding stupid figures together. After awhile, even Stevie Turcott could do it — and you know how dumb he is — but Mr. Huston, he just kept going over and over and over the stuff. Then on Friday, he told us we were gonna have to do it some more this next week!" Marty snorted again. "I hate math. I really do!"

June

The cafeteria was jammed, the air full of excited shouts as the kids at Deep River School worked off some of their last-week-of-classes energy. Tim and Marty went through the line together, then found two empty seats at one of the 4th grade tables.

"Two more days, huh?" Tim's voice was full of anticipation.

"Boy, I can't wait!"

"Me neither!" Tim looked over his shoulder. "Oh oh! There's Mr. Huston — you think he'll hassle me for not eating with the rest of my class?"

Marty shook his head. "Nah, he's in a real good mood. I guess maybe he's just as happy as we are that school's gettin' out."

Tim nodded. "Yeah, Miz Principato, too. She was real gloomy up until this week. She just kept shakin' her head and saying 'I just don't know how you children can learn if you don't apply yourselves . . .'" He raised his voice in a practiced imitation of his teacher. "She's cooled off this week, though. I guess she figures it's too late to get us all on the ball, so why worry about it?"

"Would you want to have her again next year?" Marty asked, his question somewhat garbled by a mouthful of ravioli.

Tim made a face of exaggerated disgust. "No way! Listen, you think I want to spend a whole other year making up these dumb projects and then pretending I like them?" He gulped a mouthful of food. "I learned exactly three things this year, that's all: how to clean up the room after the bell rings at 3:00, how to write neat instead of messy and how to make Miz Principato happy by telling her how exciting the class is!"

"Yeah?" Marty shrugged. "Well I wanna tell you that us kids in Mr. Huston's class are the best adders and subtracters in the school! I can even do that stuff in my head." He paused. "You know how much 39 and 26 is?"

Tim pushed a ravioli across his plate with the fork. "Uh — 55?" he responded hesitantly.

"Uh uh — it's 65!" Marty announced. "And 39 plus 42 is 81!"

Tim shrugged. "So what?"

Now it was Marty's turn to shrug. "I don't know. All I know is we learned it. We didn't learn much else, but we sure learned that!"

"So would you want to have Mr. Huston again next year?"

"No way!" Marty grimaced. "I'd rather get sick and be out of school the whole year!" Then his face took on an intensely hopeful expression. "Listen, they gotta give us somebody good next year!"

Tim bobbed his head vigorously. "You said it — and they gotta put us together in the same room, too!"

Having reached this point of clear mutual agreement, the two boys finished their lunch. Only two days to go and with luck, they felt, they could probably make it.

July

Gail Swenson, principal of the Deep River School, sat at her desk. The air conditioner was on the blink and the inside temperature had just topped 80°, but Gail wasn't thinking about the heat. She was thinking about the final batch of Achievement Test scores from the two 4th grade classes and her thoughts were less than cheerful.

How could two such different teachers achieve such equally depressing results? Oh, John Huston's kids had shone in a couple of areas — addition and subtraction, for example, but their overall math scores were still low because they had clearly failed to learn how to solve math problems and apply their skills. And Julie Principato's kids! Looking over their writing samples, Gail decided she'd never seen such a combination of good penmanship and terrible grammar, spelling and punctuation in her life!

Gail knew that both the 4th grade teachers cared about their students, and that both were intelligent, concerned teachers, but now she knew something else as well. Neither of their widely different approaches to the content of this year's 4th grade had worked. Despite their concern and commitment, the two teachers simply hadn't taught the things that the kids needed to learn and that made the kids the losers.

1

CHAPTER 1 – EXAMINING YOUR CONTENT

You Know There's More To Content Development Than Just Winging It

You take a moment to think back to some of the teachers you had when you were in school. Several of them stick in your mind. The guy whose whole philosophy seemed to be to let each of you "do your own thing," for instance. His classes were always lots of fun, full of ad-libs and interesting side-trips to discover things you had never considered before. But somehow the guy never really seemed to have it together. Each day's class was unique, totally unrelated to anything that came before or after. At the end of the year, you felt like you'd eaten too much cotton candy – stuffed and yet starving at the same time.

Then there was the teacher who did everything by the numbers. Her one aim in life seemed to be to get each of you in your seat, quiet, hands on your desk, eyes locked on her as she stood at the front of the room. She talked and you listened. She told you what to do and you did it. This wasn't like eating cotton candy – no, it was more like eating plate after plate of soggy spinach. Only you hated spinach. So every day after class you did your best to spit it out . . .

Funny – these were two different teachers but in the end they had the same effect on you. They presented impersonal content that never really had anything to do with you and your life. So in the end, the only differences they made were all negative ones.

To learn more about teaching think about teachers you have had.

By now you realize one important thing about the content you will be developing. It must be personalized in terms of your particular learners. If you're working on writing skills, you must be sure that the assignments are tailored to meet the needs of each individual in the class — not just presented for some unreal "textbook" group of children who exist only in some distant educator's imagination. Your learners will be flesh-and-blood individuals. One may have a reading problem. Another may hate math. A third may be the irrepressible class clown. You've got to take each of them — and the class as a whole — into consideration as you begin to use your content development skills.

Your skills must be personalized not just for the learners. But they must also be personalized for you! In other words, you're going to have to know how to explore every bit of content to determine where it fits, how well you understand it, what its separate parts are and so on.

Gradually you will realize that content which is not personalized for the learners reflects only the teacher's concerns — and that content which is not personalized for the teacher reflects only a hollow response to the learners' interest and enthusiasm.

Personalized Content Development Makes Order Out Of Chaos

Once again you remember your free-wheeling teacher who liked to treat each day's classes as an unexpected surprise:

"Well, here we are in the second week of November and you people are supposed to be writing paragraphs. I can tell that the idea doesn't exactly excite you. So I thought maybe we'd take today off and I'll just read you a story out of this neat book I found . . ."

By developing some new and personalized skills of your own, you're sure you can do a whole lot better than that! For one thing, you can develop the content for a whole year in terms of related units of work. And you can determine in advance exactly what topics each unit will involve. This sort of planning will help you to anticipate troublesome or monotonous areas and set up strategies for dealing with them.

No, you won't get caught off guard by a sudden attack of The Yawns among your learners and won't be confronted by a classroom that seems to be slipping towards total chaos by the minute. Your personalized content development skills will help you to be a master teacher instead of just a master ad-libber!

**Personalized Content Development Means Control By You —
Not Of You!**

"Wait a minute," you may say. "This is all very nice. But I'm afraid that this kind of systematic planning — units and tasks and the like — will just force me into a rigid structure in which I can't respond to my learners in terms of their day-to-day needs!"

This is a real and legitimate fear. No one wants to get stuck with a system in September and not see the light again until next June! But as you think things through, you will realize that personalized content development skills must be just that: skills to help you keep your content personal, meaningful and relevant to each day's classes as well as to the year as a whole. For you'll be learning to do more than plan major units and tasks. You'll also be learning to set up individual step-by-step programs to get each of your learners to the particular skills-objective you have set. And you'll be finding out too, how to deliver the particular facts, concepts and principles that comprise the supportive knowledge related to each unit.

Personalized content development skills aren't a set of rules that hold you in and control you — they're a set of practical procedures that put you in control of all the learning activities that take place in your classroom!

You find out what your learners need to learn before you teach them.

There's the list of names: Sharon Culp, Robert Bidwell, Lori James, Thomas Wyzinski . . . These are names still unattached to particular faces, names of children who may be happy or sad, bright or slow, eager or reluctant, names that will be with you for many months to come.

You'll probably be taking time to check through each of your new learners' records in the school office. You know how important it is to get some idea of each child's past work, living situation and personal idiosyncracies or interests. For the moment, however, your mind can only focus on a single, profoundly important concern.

"I want to make absolutely certain that the things I teach my kids this year are the things they really need to learn and that their learning results in new skills or skill-levels!"

You want the best for your learners. In this, you're like every truly dedicated teacher who has ever entered a classroom. In your case, however, you'll get something of a head-start. By the time you start work, you'll have the personalized content development skills you need to make good on your concern.

In your first student teaching experience, you may spend several weeks observing the supervising teacher. During that time you may find yourself increasingly eager to take your turn at teaching. Then one day it happens. Your supervising teacher turns to you and says, "You can start teaching the class tomorrow!"

Chances are that your excitement will quickly change to anxiety. You thought you were ready to teach. Now you aren't quite sure. It is your content that will give you the confidence to get up and teach. In the end, it is your content that helps you move from student to teacher.

You can begin teaching if you have a content.

Organizing and Teaching Your Content

Yes, your content is in many different places around you; when you sit down to plan a new unit, you will use all of those resources to draw that content together. You will use your content development skills to organize your material in the most efficient way to help your students learn what they need to know.

Your content is **what** you will teach your learners. You will find that content, as you look around a classroom: on the desk, the shelves, in the file cabinet, and in your briefcase. Your content will be found in textbooks, curriculum guides, a syllabus, and supplemental materials. Without your content, you would have nothing to teach. You will use your content to teach what you know about a subject so that your learners will learn that content. It is the personalized content you teach that will allow your learners to grow.

"Hey Miz James — can we learn about different kinds of animals in Science this year?"

"Yes, Wendy, we sure can. And I can tell you're pretty excited because you really want to find out about that sort of thing!"

You will use your experience as a teacher to determine what is missing in your content. Some of your learners may be deficient in content the textbook assumes they have learned. Some of your learners may be ready for more advanced content which is not defined in the curriculum guide for your grade level. So you must examine it in regard to your learners. You will not want to leave anything out of your content that your learners might need in order to grow.

Once you know what parts of your content are missing, you will find and add these missing pieces. You may ask other teachers in the building what content they have taught under similar circumstances. The curriculum supervisor may be able to give you some supplemental texts to add to your content. You may even go to your local professional library or to the Curriculum Library of a nearby university. You should explore all possible resources in order to plan the content of your new unit completely.

You can add to your content by asking others.

You will have many, many choices of content to teach. In fact, there are too many decisions to be made for you to make the right choice every time. What you must learn, therefore, is a systematic way of making these choices. **The Skills of Teaching — Content Development Skills** presents the skills of developing content so that you know HOW to write the content for effective teaching. When you understand your content, you can understand your learners' position in relation to that content. If you understand your learners, they will want to learn. And as you begin to understand how your learners feel, you start to make a difference in their lives.

"Wow, this is neat!"

"You're happy because you're learning a lot of interesting new things!"

Effective content helps you become an effective teacher.

Have You Learned All You Can?

Developing personalized content is as critical to teaching as acquisition is to learning. It is the first step of preparation that will culminate in student learning. Some teachers' content is very effective. Their students are truly learners. Over a year, these learners acquire many new skills from their teacher. And not just a few learners, either, for the truly effective teacher reaches everyone in the class. What do these teachers do that makes the difference? You may want to look at their content. What they teach will relate closely to the learners' needs and abilities. You may also find that this content is developed systematically, in learner-sized steps. Then study the teachers' lesson plans. (See **Skills of Teaching — Lesson Planning Skills**). These effective teachers will have planned to integrate their content with a variety of teaching methods, to communicate the learning to their students most efficiently. Finally, you will want to look at these teachers' interpersonal relationships with the learners (See **Skills of Teaching — Interpersonal Skills**). You will probably find that they interact with all their learners very skillfully.

Content development skills will help you to identify and organize **what** you will teach. Lesson Planning Skills will help you to define **how** you will teach the content. And Interpersonal Skills will help you **deliver** the content to your learners.

Learning to Explore, Understand and Act

It is essential for you, the teacher, to have an understanding of the learning process. Learning is your ultimate goal. You teach so that others may learn. Very simply, there are three phases of learning. The first phase involves the learners in **exploring** the new learning. Even now, as you read this material, you are exploring where you are in relation to content development skills. Taking into consideration what you already know about personalized content development, you are exploring what else you might need to learn. Once you determine what you already know, the next phase is to **understand** what you need to know. When you explore the skills of content development, you will understand the function of these new skills more fully. When you understand how the new pieces fit with the old ones, you are ready for the third phase of learning: **acting**. When you **explore** what you know and **understand** what you need to know, then you can **act** to write your content.

PHASES OF LEARNING

		I	II	III
LEARNER:	**LEARNING SKILLS**	Exploring what you know	Understanding what you need to know	Acting with what you have learned

10   Helping the Learners to Explore, Understand and Act

The learners can be taught most effectively when you help them **explore** the new learning first. You can give them an opportunity to explore what they know and do not know about the new learning. As your learners explore you may hear them say:

"What's this called?"

"What does this do?"

"Is this right?"

In the second phase, you can help your learners **understand** what they do not know. The more the learners understand, the more often you will hear them say:

"This goes here!"

"I see how this works now!"

"I think I can do it!"

Finally, you will help the learners to **act** in the last phase of learning. You will hear them say:

"I can do that!"

"It's my turn!"

"Look at mine!"

Helping your learners to **explore, understand** and **act** will maximize your success with teaching and your learners' success with learning.

If your learners explore, understand, and act, they will be successful.

Interpersonal skills are the teaching skills of delivery. Bridging the gap between the content and the learners, they make the difference between teachers who relate the content effectively and those who do not. Consider attending, the first set of interpersonal skills. You use attending skills with the learners before they begin to explore. Placing yourself in such a way that you may attend to all of them, you may circulate around the room. You make eye contact with each member of the group. Most importantly, when you speak with the learners, you approach and face them squarely, observing and listening fully to what they say.

PHASES OF LEARNING

PRE-LEARNING

		I	II	III
TEACHER:	INTERPERSONAL SKILLS	Attending		
LEARNER:	LEARNING SKILLS	Exploring what you know ▶	Understanding what you need to know ▶	Acting with what you have learned

12 Attending Involves the Learners in Learning

There are many ways to attend to your learners. Positioning yourself in relation to the learners communicates your interest in them. Attending prepares you to receive information about the learners just by watching and listening to what is happening in the classroom. By communicating and watching, you are equipped to involve the learners in a learning experience. When using attending skills, you will find yourself thinking:

"Rachel is staring out the window again! Maybe she needs some help."

"Whatever is Kenneth doing wandering around the room! Does he have all his materials?"

"Jason has finished, so I'll get him started on the reading."

If you attend to the learners, you will be able to involve them fully in the learning.

Responding

You should not only attend to the learners, but respond to them as well. When you use responding skills in your delivery, you help the learners to explore. Responding skills help you enter the learners' frames of reference and thus give you an idea of where they are "coming from." These skills reveal to you and to the learners what they know and do not know. If all learning begins with the learners' frames of reference, then it is only appropriate to employ responding skills to enter those frames of reference. An effective teacher will shy away from sermonizing ("It's your own fault you haven't learned your number facts") and respond to the learners ("You get frustrated because you have to count on your fingers"). This second response communicates a real understanding of the learners and their experience. Then the learners may be motivated to learn the number facts; not because you have told them to but because they know you understand their experience of the learning task. They will feel better when they do not have to count on their fingers anymore.

PHASES OF LEARNING

PRE-LEARNING

		I	II	III
TEACHER:	**INTERPERSONAL SKILLS**	Attending ▶ Responding		
LEARNER:	**LEARNING SKILLS**	Exploring ▶	Understanding ▶	Acting

Attending skills prepare you to respond to the learners. Responding skills help your learners to explore what they know and what they do not know. As your learners attack new skills, you will respond to their feelings and the content of what they say. You may respond: "You all feel pretty good about doing this experiment but aren't quite sure how to describe it." You may hear the learners explore the task when they say:

"Experiments are fun to do but the reports are hard!"

"What do you write down first?"

"I never know where to begin!"

Then the learners are ready for more of your teaching skills.

If you respond, you will help your learners explore new learning.

Personalizing

In addition to attending and responding, you need personalizing skills. When you personalize for your learners, they understand more of what they need to learn. Your responding skills have let you enter your learners' frames of reference so that you can personalize the new learning for the learners. You not only see the learning situation through your learners' eyes, but you relate the students' experiences to the learning tasks. You personalize the learners' experiences of the learning tasks so that they will understand their individual learning goals.

PHASES OF LEARNING

		PRE-LEARNING	I	II	III
TEACHER:	INTERPERSONAL SKILLS	Attending	Responding	Personalizing	
LEARNER:	LEARNING SKILLS		Exploring	Understanding	Acting

Having responded to the learners in the exploration phase of learning, you will move toward personalizing in the understanding phase of learning. You may say: "You feel mixed-up because you don't know when to start a new sentence." Then your learners can understand what they need to know and may respond to you as they begin to understand.

"I just don't know where to put the period."

"It seems okay to me, but you marked it wrong!"

"How are you supposed to do it?"

If you personalize, you will be able to help your learners to understand the new learning.

Initiating

In the last phase of teaching delivery, you will use initiating skills. You facilitate the learners' ability to act to learn what they need to know. To do that, you systematically break the learning down into steps. These steps are written in such a way that your learners can manage them: not too large, not too small. You develop programs that include the learners' goals: "Your goal is to begin learning the '2' number facts." You develop programs that include a first step that comes from the learners' frames of reference: "Your first step is to describe what you were trying to prove in the experiment." You develop the remaining steps to reach the learning goal: "These are the five steps you should take to write a good, complete sentence."

PHASES OF LEARNING

PRE-LEARNING

			I	II	III
TEACHER:	**INTERPERSONAL SKILLS**	Attending ▶	Responding ⬇	Personalizing ⬇	Initiating ⬇
LEARNER:	**LEARNING SKILLS**		Exploring ↗	Understanding ↗	Acting

With increased initiating skills, the quality of your learners' action will improve considerably. When the learners act, they recycle the phases of learning using the feedback they get. They **explore** the relationship between the parts of what they are doing; they **understand** a new concept of how these parts fit together; they prepare to **act** again to test the new ideas. When you initiate with programs derived from your learners' frames of reference, you ensure their success in the active phase of learning. And as they act, you may hear them say:

"So that's why there are shells in the rock!"

"I wonder what would happen if I put some vinegar on this rock?"

"See! We did it! It's limestone!"

If you initiate the right steps for your learners, they will be able to act.

Personalizing Content means Understanding Your Learners

"It's the first week in November, so my kids must be ready to learn about long division."

Sound familiar? You may have known a few teachers who tended to let their content and its pattern of organization run their classes. By now, however, you know that this sort of approach to content development is self-defeating. Content that does not spring from an awareness of each learners' unique frames of reference is an impersonal one. And impersonal content does little for real living, breathing and learning people!

You must personalize the content from the start, thinking: "My kids may get confused by the shift from single-digit to multiple-digit multiplication — so I'll build in a special step to include work on remainders." Or "Late January is usually the slowest, dullest time of the year for kids this age so I'll make sure to spend a week on something really exciting — something that'll get them moving around."

You need to do more than just develop content. You need to personalize your content, to promote as much active, involved and successful learning as possible!

Personalizing with Learners helps them Deal Constructively with Your Content

"You didn't do too well on this writing assignment, Jimmy. You'll have to work harder if you're going to do well."

Inspiring? Or just another depressing pep-talk — the kind kids get tired of hearing? The latter, of course. You know that this sort of impersonal advice won't help your learners to master the content, and you should know as well, that the best approach to learner problems — or triumphs — is a truly personalized one.

"You're really bugged with yourself because you can't figure out the math."

"Hey, Tony, you're really on top of the world because you aced that test, huh?"

"Margie, you seem pretty sad because you can't find another book as good as that last one."

Personalizing your content for learners. And personalizing with learners to help them master this content. These are the key ingredients in **personalized** content development. For a thorough introduction to the specific interpersonal skills involved, read **The Skills Of Teaching: Interpersonal Skills**. For now, however, just remember that content is only effective when its development and delivery have involved your personalizing skills!

Organizing what you will teach and how you will teach it requires several sets of skills. One of these sets of skills will enable you to develop content for the learners. The content is what the learners will explore, understand and act on. Without it there is nothing to learn. Developing the units, topics or tasks that the learners will learn over the year in your class, is the first step of content development. Following this, you must break each task content into the skills needed to perform it. In addition, you will identify the supportive knowledge that the learners will need to perform the skills.

PHASES OF LEARNING

		PRE-LEARNING	I	II	III
LEARNER:	**LEARNING SKILLS**		Exploring	Understanding	Acting
TEACHER:	**PREPARATION SKILLS**	Developing Content			

Whether your content is in the form of a prescribed curriculum or a textbook series, you must evaluate that content. You will modify the existing content to fit the needs of your learners. You may say to yourself: "My learners need to learn how to spell. Adding prefixes and suffixes are things that they will have to do too." As you break these tasks into individual skills, you may say "Adding 'ing' to a word with a long vowel and silent 'e' will be the first skill. The steps are: 1) consonant-vowel-consonant-'e' word, 2) drop silent 'e', 3) add 'ing'." Finally, you will determine what supportive knowledge the learners may need: "I'll want to make sure the learners know the long vowel sounds!" Developing content in this manner is a step toward learner exploration.

When you develop your content, keep your learners' needs in mind.

Developing Content

In the course of a school year, you will teach many different kinds of things. Some of the things you teach will be in your specialty area. Some may not, but will concern areas that are unfamiliar to you. Some of your lessons may be effective ("I'm really doing it, aren't I Mr. Jones?"), others may not ("Wow — I'm really lost!"). Your success depends in large part upon how well you develop your content.

We will ask you now to develop your content in your specialty subject area. Simply take a small piece of the content that you intend to teach. We realize that we cannot ask you for a comprehensive curriculum or syllabus. Time does not permit this. At a minimum, however, take 20 or 30 minutes to **write out an outline of the content of one lesson** you wish to deliver. After you become an expert in making judgments about what constitutes effective content development, you will be able to return and give your content a rating.

Develop your content exactly as you would prepare it for a class you were going to teach. Please include the following content development objectives in your content:

First, show how this material fits into the year's content, including the course title, the unit, and the part of the unit that this lesson is taken from.

Second, describe what your learners should have learned previous to this lesson.

Third, list the skill you will teach.

Fourth, list all the steps needed to perform the new skill.

Fifth, define any terms or facts the learners may need to understand in order to perform the steps.

Content Outline of One Lesson:

In spite of all the teacher-training you may have had, you probably had some difficulty in producing some of the content. Most teacher-training programs emphasize learning to discriminate or critique — not doing or producing. However, you may feel that they have also taught you how to recognize the merits of good content development as opposed to poor development.

We will now give you an opportunity to get an index of your current ability to make accurate judgments about effective content development. Being able to make accurate judgments or discriminations concerning what it is that constitutes effective content development skills will contribute to your being able to develop your own content. You will receive immediate feedback on your ability to discriminate.

We are going to present you with five different levels of content developed by teachers. All of these contents have attempted to meet the requirements of the assignment which you have just completed. Rate each of the contents presented from 1.0 to 5.0 as follows:

1.0 — Very Ineffective

2.0 — Ineffective

3.0 — Minimally Effective

4.0 — Very Effective

5.0 — Extremely Effective

If you feel a content falls between two levels on a five-point scale, you may rate it as 1.5, 2.5, 3.5 or 4.5. You may use a rating more than once.

Your Rating:_____

Course Title: MATHEMATICS

     Unit: Decimal Fractions

   Topics: Addition of Decimal Fractions

    Task: Understanding Place Value

    Skill: Reading Decimals to the Hundredths Place

1) The place to the right of the decimal point is called the tenths place.
   a) Decimal points — separate whole numbers from fractional numbers
   b) Right — ➤
   c) Tenths — ?/10

2) Read the digit and name the place.
   a) Digit — 0-9 numerals
   b) Place — spaces to the right or left of the decimal point

3) The place two spaces to the right of the decimal point is called the hundredths place.
   a) Hundredths — ?/100

4) Read the numeral and name the place. (Numeral — combination of digits that name a number).

5) Write a fraction that expresses the name of the decimal and ask yourself if that is its correct name.
   a) If you can name the place values of decimal fractions, then you can always have a common denominator by adding zero place holders.

Your Rating:————————————————————————

Course Title: SOCIAL STUDIES

   Unit: Geography of North America

 Topic: Natural Resources

  Task: Map Reading

  Skill: United States

1) Coastal Area
   a) Fishing — 4 million tons a year
   b) Lumbering — wood, pulp, and paper
   c) Petroleum and Natural Gas
   d) Sulfur — 50% of world's supply

2) Piedmont Area
   a) Coal — West Va. leads production
   b) Zinc
   c) Bauxite
   d) Phosphate
   e) Lumbering
   f) Water Power

3) Mountain Area
   a) Copper — 1/5 of the world's copper
   b) Iron — open pit mining
   c) Lead — Missouri, Idaho and Utah
   d) Uranium — needed for atomic energy
   e) Lumbering — Rocky Mountains
   f) Water Power

4) Plains Area
   a) Farming — produce surplus
   b) Coal — undeveloped reserves
   c) Petroleum and Natural Gas

Your Rating:_____

Course Title: HANDWRITING

    Unit: Manuscript Letters

   Topic: Horizontal and Vertical Lines

    Task: Capital Letters

    Skill: Printing E, F and H

1) Print E following model.
    a) One vertical line (straight up and down)
    b) Three horizontal lines (straight left to right)

2) Print F following model.
    a) One vertical line
    b) Two horizontal lines

3) Print H following model.
    a) Two vertical lines
    b) One horizontal line

4) If your vertical lines are truly vertical, your letters will stand at attention.

5) If your horizontal lines are truly horizontal, they will look strong and solid.

CONTENT D

Your Rating: —————————————————————

Course Title: GENERAL SCIENCE

    Unit: The Human Body

  Topic: Digestion

   Task: The Food Passage

  Skill: Major Organs in the Alimentary Canal and the Role They Play in Digestion

1) Mouth
   a) Teeth bite and grind
   b) Tongue kneads (pushes together)
   c) Saliva moistens

2) Esophagus — carries food to stomach

3) Stomach
   a) Secretes gastric juices
   b) Churns food
   c) Pylorus — valve at end of stomach before small intestines

4) Small Intestines (22-25 ft. long)
   a) Secretes digestive juices
   b) Villi — absorb food into blood and lymph

5) Large Intestine
   a) Secretes mucus
   b) Absorbs water into body
   c) Excretes waste

6) If you can name the organs and their function, then you will be able to trace food from the moment it is eaten, until it enters the blood stream.

Your Rating:_____

Course Title: READING — LEVEL 3

    Unit: Phonics

   Topic: Vowel Sounds

    Task: Short Vowels

   Skill: 'e'

1) Copy following list.
   a) Eat
   b) Egg
   c) Elephant
   d) Eager
   e) Envy

2) Identify those words that begin with short 'e'.

3) Write three words that have a short 'e' middle sound.

4) Spell the following words using short 'e'.
   a) Beg
   b) Bet
   c) Pest
   d) Nest
   e) Neck
   f) Deck

You may have had some difficulty distinguishing among a few of the contents. Perhaps some were perfectly clear to you. In any event, you will want to know, in general, how well you did. In this way you will get a feeling for the personal learning and growth that the remainder of this book will deliver to you.

The contents you have just rated were varied according to different levels of development. Effectively developed content includes all of the steps and knowledge required to perform the skill. Only **one** of these contents had **all** of the steps and knowledge necessary for learner performance. When a teacher has developed all of the steps and knowledge needed to perform the skill, the learners can be involved in a process that enables them to achieve the goal.

By now you may be eager to get some kind of an idea of how well you did in rating the content. We will give you feedback on your ability to discriminate effective from ineffective content.

Trained raters, who have demonstrated the validity of their ratings in studies on teaching outcome, rated each of the contents in terms of its level of development. These ratings are listed in the table below, by which you may determine your discrimination score.

Content	Ratings
A	5.0
B	1.0
C	4.0
D	3.0
E	2.0

You may use the table of ratings as follows:

1. Without regard to whether the differences are positive or negative, write down the difference between each of your numerical ratings and each of those of the trained raters.

2. Add up the difference scores. You should have five of them since there were five contents.

3. Divide the total of the difference scores you obtained in step 2, by the total number of ratings, 5. The resulting number is your discrimination score.

Here is an illustration:

Content	Ratings		Sample Ratings		Difference (Deviation from Ratings)
A	5.0	-	2.0	=	3.0
B	1.0	-	2.0	=	1.0
C	4.0	-	3.0	=	1.0
D	3.0	-	1.0	=	2.0
E	2.0	-	2.0	=	0.0

$$\text{TOTAL} = \frac{7.0}{5} = 1.4 \quad \text{Content Development Discrimination Score}$$

Your Score:

Content	Ratings		Your Ratings		Difference (Deviation from Ratings)
A	5.0	-	_____	=	_____
B	1.0	-	_____	=	_____
C	4.0	-	_____	=	_____
D	3.0	-	_____	=	_____
E	2.0	-	_____	=	_____

$$\text{TOTAL} = \frac{\_\_\_\_}{5} = \_\_\_\_ \quad \text{Pre-Training Content Development Discrimination Score}$$

The average teacher who has not had systematic teaching skills, usually differs from one (1.0) to one and one-half (1.5) levels from the ratings of the trained raters. This is really not so good since it means that while a trained rater may rate a content at level 3.0, you might rate that item at 4.5 or 1.5. You are rating as "highly effective" or "highly ineffective" content that trained raters rate as "minimally effective." Generally, teachers tend to be furthest from the given ratings in their judgment of content which is most abstract or conceptual. These contents only appear to include the effective dimensions of content development.

One-half level (.5) deviation from the trained raters' rating is considered a good discrimination score. It means that while the trained rater rates an item at level 3.0, you might rate it between 2.5 and 3.5. When you have completed the work in this book, you should deviate by one-half level or less from the trained raters' rating!

Perhaps you are ready now for a further exploration of the rating system. You may wish to have at least a tentative understanding of how the ratings were made. This explanation will also serve as preliminary training in content development. Later, you will receive more extensive training.

Independent of how a lesson will be delivered, one of the essential ingredients of an effective lesson is comprehensive identification of the content. In the case of Content A, the mathematics skill the students are expected to learn is fully broken into procedural steps needed to correctly perform the skill. It identifies the names of these things involved in doing the skill, and what each of them does. The outline also includes a way for the learners to evaluate their own work and an application of the skills, and thus, it deserves its 5.0 rating.

Content C (4.0) includes all of the relevant information about its handwriting content, including the proper labels, their meanings and why this skill is important. It falls short, however, because it does not include the steps the learners need to be able to write the letters. Content D similarly identifies the informational components of a general science learning, but fails to qualify as a skill. Recall of facts and concepts is **not** a skill, nor can the learners be given steps to recall those terms every time. The outline is, therefore, given a rating of 3.0.

For its 2.0 rating, Content E included the functions of reading and spelling using short 'e', but did not give the steps or a reason for doing the skill. Without these, the content is a series of random exercises which may 'hit or miss.' Content B (1.0) is very ineffective because this social studies content is chiefly concerned with labels or factual information.

Yes! There is much to learn about teaching — preparation and delivery involve many skills. **But before you can write a lesson plan or teach a lesson, you should begin to learn how to break your content down into pieces.** Your success in developing personalized content depends on your knowing all the parts of each unit you teach. "Hey, we really learned **everything** about frogs, didn't we?"

"We sure did, Mike — and you're excited to find out how much you could really learn!"

First, you will learn how to break that unit into topics. If the unit is multiplication, two possible topics would be the multiplication of whole numbers and the multiplication of fractional numbers. Next, there should be several tasks within each topic. If the unit concerns the writing of a paragraph, and one of the topics is writing a complete sentence, then identifying subjects and predicates are two tasks of that topic. Then you break the tasks into the skills that the learners need to perform, so that they can accomplish the tasks. Then they can master the topic and complete the unit. For example, in order to identify the predicate, your learners may need to learn the skill of identifying action verbs.

Developing the Daily Content

A skill is what you teach in one class period. You begin to develop your daily content by breaking that skill down into steps. If your daily skill is finding the product of two 3-digit numbers, you will want to tell your learners how to do that skill, step-by-step. In addition, you will develop the supportive knowledge the learners will need to perform the steps correctly. You may have to show your learners a 'spring balance' so that they will know what to use for weighing their samples in the laboratory. Perhaps you need to explain what 'parallel' means if the lesson requires it. The learners may need to know why they should break new spelling words into syllables. Your daily content should include all the information the learners need to acquire the day's skill. If it does, you won't hear "Well, maybe I can do it" but "Yeah! Now I **know** I can do it!"

When you teach skills, your learners can grow.

CHAPTER TWO: DEVELOPING YOUR YEARLY CONTENT

Yesterday

"Boy, am I ever glad school is finally over! I think if I'd had to go one more day, I'd have thrown up!"

"Tracey, that's no way to talk — "

"Oh Mom, I just hated this whole year. I thought I was going to like it but it was just — **yucky**!"

"Well, I know you haven't been very happy about school this year. What do you think was wrong? Why did it go so badly?"

"Oh, that's easy — it was that dumb Mr. Wexsler! He didn't teach us anything. He didn't even care about us! It was like all he cared about the whole year was his stupid schedule!"

"Really, Tracy, I —"

"I mean it! He didn't even care that half us kids couldn't pass his dumb tests. He never explained or anything! He just kept going. I hated the whole school year — and Mr. Wexsler most of all!"

SOME TEACHERS DEVELOP A WHOLE YEAR'S CONTENT WITHOUT REALLY TAKING THE LEARNERS INTO CONSIDERATION.

Have you ever stopped to think how the content is determined for any course that you might teach? As a student teacher, you assume your cooperating teacher's experience produces an effective content. Certainly with several years experience, all teachers should know what they want to teach and what they don't. Right? **Wrong!** Experienced teachers too will look for direction from the supervisor or administration as to what content to teach. That content may take the form of a detailed content outline including goals and objectives. It may simply entail the use of a textbook series or several different textbooks. Sometimes, the decision of what content to teach is made on the basis of past experience.

"We'll teach the same content this year as we did last year."

Judging Your Content's Completeness

This is not to say that last year's content has to be altered for this year's learners. Change for change's sake is not effective teaching. What you need at this point, is a way to develop and evaluate the content you will be given to teach. You will want to judge the content's completeness, and determine what, if any, necessary content is missing. You will require a perspective on the content to be taught over the year. Above all, you will want to avoid a negative judgment from the people who really count the most — your learners.

"She's always so confusing . . ."

"He didn't teach me anything . . ."

"She just didn't care about the kids in her class . . ."

If your content is complete, then the learners will trust you.

Someday you may be asked to be a member of a curriculum committee. If you are already teaching, you may have already had this opportunity. In most cases, the committee will be composed of several experienced teachers and a supervisor. The committee will have a number of meetings to establish its guidelines and to gather input. And before anyone realizes it, the deadline is rapidly approaching and SOMETHING must be done! "We have to have our curriculum done by next week so that we can order the materials on this year's budget," you may be told. In the ensuing panic, a number of sample textbooks will be thrown onto the table. Somehow, one is never quite sure how, a series is selected for adoption. How will the learners react? "Hey, this book is super!" Or, if you choose less well, "What a yucky book — I hate it!" For better or worse, the book's table of contents will become the curriculum; but the members of the committee are happy that they will not be bothered with any more afternoon meetings.

When you learn the skills of content development, you will be better equipped to select a textbook. You will be able to take that table of contents and add the content your learners need in addition to those in the text. Your content development skills are the first step toward effective teaching.

If you can select the right textbook, then the learners will be able to learn from you and their texts.

Attempting to Develop Content

The content that you develop will be as varied as the subjects you teach and the learners who study these materials. Indeed, a good teacher will vary the content within a subject area more than a poor teacher will in a number of subject areas. This is what makes learning from a good teacher so exciting. Whatever content good teachers organize, they follow certain common rules. They realize that the way one organizes content is critical to the learners' grasp of that material. Content development is a key to effective teaching.

"I really learned a lot this year, Ms. Smith!"

"You feel really happy with yourself because you were able to handle all the material we covered!"

Before you begin this chapter on developing your yearly content, you may want to examine your own skills in this area. The simplest way to do this, is to organize the content in your own specialty area. Why don't you try this right now? Just think of a subject you would like to teach. Select a grade level at which you could teach it. Then outline what would constitute a quarter of a year's content in this subject. Please take at least 30 minutes to outline this content before proceeding through this chapter.

The pre-training assessment in Chapter One asked you to outline the content of a single lesson, and then to show how it would fit into the year's content plan. This assessment asks you to outline the content for a quarter of a year.

Using Models for Developing Content

In order to provide an on-going illustration of two points — that these skills can be mastered, and that such mastery makes a difference — let us introduce Sandra Greer and her class.

Sandra could easily be a teacher in the 4th or 6th grade, in a junior high, senior high, or even in college. For as we see, what matters most is not the age or grade taught, but what the students learn — and what Sandra herself learns.

"All right," Sandra muttered. "Let me examine my English curriculum. I'll outline what I'm planning to teach next quarter!"

I.   English — Level A

    A. Parts of Speech — nouns and verbs
    B. Sentences — subject and predicate
    C. Spelling — phonic rules
    D. Punctuation — period, comma, colon, semi-colon
    E. Dictionary Skills — syllables and meaning
    F. Usage — singular and plural
    G. Paragraphs — opening sentence, body, concluding sentence
    H. Short Stories — who, what, when, where, why, how
    I. Poetry — rhymes and meter
    J. Book Reports — written and oral

You may have found that it is not easy to develop a content outline in such a brief time. You may also realize how critical content development skills are. The kind of content that you develop will determine what you teach and how you teach it. As critical as these skills are, no one has ever taught you how to get an index of your current ability to make judgments about effective content development. Being able to make accurate judgments or discriminations concerning effective content development will contribute to your own content development skills. You will receive immediate feedback on your ability to discriminate the level of content development. After the content development training, you will be able to rate your own content.

In the second part of this pre-training assessment you will have a chance to rate a series of contents. Although these may not address your grade level or your subject matter, use what you know about content development to evaluate them. Please rate each of these Learning Contents from 1.0 to 5.0 as follows:

1.0 – Very Ineffective

2.0 – Ineffective

3.0 – Minimally Effective

4.0 – Very Effective

5.0 – Extremely Effective

If you feel a content falls between two levels on the five-point scale, you may rate it as 1.5, 2.5, 3.5, or 4.5. For example, if a content seemed to you to be somewhere between 'minimally effective' and 'very effective,' you would give it a 3.5. You may use a rating more than once.

Your Rating:_____

Mathematics — Level 3

I. Using Counting Numbers
    A. Understanding Place Values
        1.Ordering the numbers
            a. Using "greater than"
            b. Using "less than"
        2. Using money
            a. Counting pennies
            b. Counting dimes
        3. Naming two, three and four-digit numbers
            a. Naming numerals orally
            b. Writing numerals from words
    B. Addition and Subtraction
        1. Understanding the concepts
            a. Combining numbers
            b. Taking away from numbers
        2. Solving equations
            a. Finding N when $a + N = b$
            b. Finding N when $N + a = b$
            c. Finding N when $a + b = N$
            d. Finding N when $N - a = b$
            e. Finding N when $a - N = b$
            f. Finding N when $a - b = N$

II. Using Geometry
    A. Understanding Points, Lines, and Segments
        1. Constructing line segments
            a. Constructing triangles
            b. Constructing quadrilaterals
            c. Constructing polygons
        2. Constructing Diagonals
            a. Constructing diagonals of triangles
            b. Constructing diagonals of quadrilaterals
            c. Constructing diagonals of polygons
    B. Understanding Angles
        1. Measuring right angles
            a. Finding the right angle of a right triangle
            b. Finding the right angles of a rectangle
            c. Finding the right angles of a square
        2. Measuring acute and obtuse angles
            a. Naming the angles of an equilateral triangle
            b. Naming the angles of a parallelogram
            c. Naming the angles of a rhombus

CONTENT B

Your Rating:_____

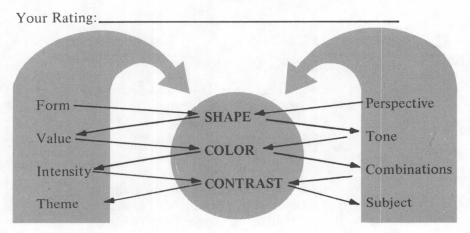

Your Rating:_____

I. English — Level A

    A. Parts of Speech — nouns and verbs

    B. Sentences — subjects and predicates

    C. Spelling — phonetic rules

    D. Punctuation — period, comma, colon, semi-colon

    E. Dictionary Skills — syllables and meaning

    F. Usage — singular and plural

    G. Paragraphs — opening sentence, body, concluding sentence

    H. Short Stories — who, what, when, where, why, how

    I. Poetry — rhymes and meter

    J. Book Reports — written and oral

Your Rating: _____

Level 5 — Reading

I. Improving Comprehension

    A. Reading Critically
        1. Recognizing main idea
        2. Recognizing story problems and solution
        3. Recognizing organization of ideas

II. Improving Fluency

    A. Using Written Language
        1. Recognizing alphabetical order
        2. Discriminating visual patterns
        3. Using picture cues

    B. Using Spoken Language
        1. Recognizing semantic cues
        2. Discriminating auditory patterns
        3. Using letter-sound relationship cues

Your Rating:_____

United States History

Early Colonization
Tracing Indian Civilization
Mapping Early Exploration and Settlement
Contrasting the Thirteen Colonies

Americans Win Independence
Understanding the Conflict with England
Tracing the Birth of a Nation
Framing the Constitution

Westward Expansion
Following the Early Settlers in the Mississippi Valley
Understanding the War of 1812
Mapping the Southwest and California

A Growing Nation
Analyzing the Industrial Revolution
Understanding Life in the North
Comparing Life in the South

A Divided Nation
Understanding States Rights and Slavery
Following the Civil War
Following the Reconstruction of the South

Growing Cities
Tracing the Machine Age
Understanding the Workers and the Farmers
Comparing Immigration and the City

A World Power
Going Beyond the Borders
Following the Progressive Era
Understanding World War I

Social and Economic Change
Understanding the Jazz Age
Following the Depression and the New Deal
Tracing World War II

That was a difficult pre-test for many of you! At some level, the contents all look somewhat alike. Yet you know there are differences. You still can't quite say why they are different though, because no one has ever taught you how to do this.

You may want to get some idea of how you did in demonstrating your content development skills. Your score will tell you how well you have discriminated effective from ineffective content development.

Trained raters, who have demonstrated the validity of their ratings in studies on teaching outcome, rated each of the contents according to the level of content development skills employed. These ratings are listed in the table below.

You may use the table of ratings to determine your own discrimination score, by obtaining the difference between each of your ratings and those of the trained raters. Add these differences, and divide by 5 to determine your yearly content organization discrimination score.

Content	Ratings	Your Ratings	Difference
A	5.0	- _____	= _____
B	1.0	- _____	= _____
C	2.0	- _____	= _____
D	4.0	- _____	= _____
E	3.0	- _____	= _____
		TOTAL = _____	= _____

$$\frac{}{5}$$

Pre-training
Yearly Content
Discrimination
Score

Understanding the Rating Scale

One of the principles of effective teaching, is to provide as much feedback as possible in each step of the learning program. You may wish to have at least a tentative understanding of how the ratings were determined. An explanation will also serve as preliminary training in yearly content organization. A rating of 5.0 means that the content was broken into five levels of detail. The Mathematics content was rated most complete because it included: 1) title of the **course**, 2) Roman Numerals — the **units**, 3) capital letters — the chapters, sections, or **topics**, 4) Arabic Numerals — the **tasks**, and 5) small letters — the daily **skills**. The next most complete content was the Reading content, which received a rating of 4.0. It failed to be as complete as the Mathematics content because it did not break the tasks into daily skills. For example, under the last task, "using letter-sound relationship cues," are ultimately all of the phonetic rules. Content E rated 3.0 because it included three levels of general content: the course, the units, and the topics. Sandra's content C rated only a 2.0 because she included only two levels of content detail. The Art content (1.0) was very incomplete because it failed even to tell you what course it was intended to describe.

Now you are ready to go back and rate the content that you developed at the beginning of this chapter. Determine how many levels of detail you included. Did you name the course (1.0)? Did you name at least two units (2.0)? Did you list topics under each unit (3.0)? Did you list tasks under each topic (4.0)? Did you list the daily skills under each task (5.0)? These ratings do not take into account the quality of the developed content. The quality of the content you develop would have to be evaluated by your instructor or supervisor. However, it is possible for you to rate your content quantitatively as you have just done.

Your Pre-Training Communication Score: _____

Needless to say, Sandra was not overjoyed to discover that her general content was rated at 2.0. How in the world could she be so dumb! "Well, I had to start some place," she thought. "And it's better to start at the bottom. The only place to go is up!" Looking back over her content, she had a strong hunch that she had done what most well-intentioned but largely unskilled teachers had done before her. "I can list all sorts of units to teach. The more shopping bags the better!" Sandra continued to analyze her content. "Then I can put whatever I want into the bags, depending on my mood. It's comfortable to leave the door open by not putting too much detail down in the content."

To her credit, Sandra squarely faced the truth about herself. She really wanted to make a difference in her kids' lives this year — and to do this, she now realized she would have to concentrate as never before.

Not "Ms. Greer, what're we supposed to be doing; And not "Ms. Greer, I'm really lost!"

But "Gee, Ms. Greer, I really did it right, huh?" So that Sandra could answer "And you feel just great because you can do it!"

To develop your yearly content, you will need to organize what you will teach into at least five levels. There is no magic to the number five. That number just insures a level of detail that is needed for effective teaching. To develop the five levels of your content, you will start to organize the content beginning with the name of **the course** or subject. Then you will list **the units** you plan to teach during the year. From each unit you will organize **the topics** or sections that the unit should include for your course. Under each topic you will write **the tasks** that the sections need. Finally, you will write **the daily skills** needed to complete these tasks.

The chart below illustrates this organization of the year's content. To develop the content, work from left to right. To deliver it, you will move in the opposite direction, starting with the skills.

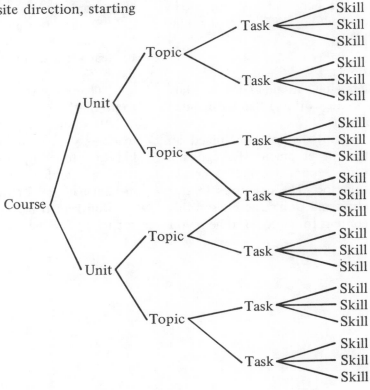

You are ready now, to begin reading about how you should organize your yearly content. But that is not enough. Besides reading about them, you must **use** these content development skills. Unless you implement what you are studying, acquisition of the new skills will not take place. That is why each step of content development is accompanied by an **exercise** for the reader to perform. To help you with these exercises, we have included content examples taken from the work of Sandra and her fellow teacher, Don Roberts. Sandra and Don take their jobs seriously. They care about the children in their classes. Effective teaching is each one's personal goal. Both teachers constantly re-evaluate their skills delivery in relation to the students.

Sandra noticed last year that her students' growth in math skills was less than she had hoped — and the kids recognized the problem too.

"Ms Greer, I just can't do it!"

"Listen, this stuff is just too hard!"

Sandra knew her learners felt stupid because they couldn't make sense of their math work, so Sandra decided to take a closer look at her content.

At about this time, the school district announced an in-service workshop on content development. Recognizing her own math content problem, Sandra decided to enroll. She talked Don into signing up, too. The examples in this book are excerpted from Sandra's and Don's exercises in this workshop. You can use their content for a model to help you perform the assigned exercises.

Don had a unique kind of problem. Having taught for over five years, he was considered by most of his former students to be a great teacher. But this year, Don had twenty-five "free spirits" for students. One could hardly call them learners.

"What a collection," Don exclaimed to Sandra. "I've had some tough kids before, but never a group like this one! They can't sit still or keep quiet for one minute. It's impossible for me to teach!"

He continued to describe his students' disruptive behavior: "It isn't that they're bad kids — one at a time, they're great. But all together . . ." His voice trailed off and his eyeballs rolled back in his head. "You just wouldn't believe the group's dynamics, Sandy!"

"Sounds terrible," responded Sandra shaking her head. "You must feel really frustrated because you want to be able to teach those kids, but they don't even know how to listen!"

"That's right! I'd have to shout them down, and I refuse to do that!"

"It sounds like you're saying that before you even begin teaching your academic curriculum, you have to teach these kids how to learn," Sandra summarized Don's problem. "You need a learning content! Sounds like you could use this in-service course I'm taking on Wednesdays."

Don leaned forward. "That's it, Sandy! That is what I've got to do for these kids. They have to learn HOW . . . TO . . . LEARN!"

One of the first steps to take when developing your content is to identify the course or subject that would include this area of study. You may be developing your content for fifth grade mathematics, or eighth grade social studies. You may be using a specific textbook as a guideline for your subject, or developing your content from scratch. In either case, the subject or **course** is the title of the content outline you will develop.

If you identify the title of your content, then the learners will know where the goal line is.

Don was developing a content to teach his learners how to learn. He was, so to speak, developing a content from scratch. But first, he had to decide what area of study would include this content. After thinking through his schedule, he decided that Social Studies would be an appropriate subject in which to learn "how to learn." Sandra on the other hand, wanted to practice her content development skills using a Mathematics text. The title of Don's course is Social Studies — Level 6, while Sandra's course is entitled Mathematics C.

Course: Social Studies — 6   Course: Mathematics C

Naming Your Content

You are ready to select a content to be developed in an ongoing manner throughout this book. You will use this content in each of the practice exercises. These exercises will involve you in breaking this content down into finer and more specific detail. Select a course with which you are familiar and at a level that you might teach. It would be helpful for you to have available one or more textbooks you might use to teach the course you have selected. They will serve as a point of reference as you develop the content. Now write the name of the course you have selected as a title for your content outline.

Course:_____

After determining what the course is, you are ready to define the units you will teach over the year in that course. Units are the large divisions of the course. There should be at least two units to a course. Probably, your course will have more than two. For example, you may want to divide your language arts content into four units: spelling, grammar, writing paragraphs and reading. But there are no set rules which say that this is the only way to organize language arts. That is because the learners in different situations have their special needs. Another teacher may select three units for the learners: reading, writing and speaking. Each set of units is as potentially effective as the other. That is because each unit will be divided into three more levels. And when each content is complete in respect to the learners, these units could very well contain identical elements, appearing in a different sequence, however.

Another way to determine the units of your content, is to look at the table of contents in your course's textbooks. Where several chapters are grouped under one heading, you have the name of a unit. You may have to examine several textbooks before you find this level of detail in the table of contents.

If you break the course into units, then the learners will be able to organize what they learn.

Don already knew that one of his units was learning skills. To complete the units in his social studies course, he looked at the table of contents in two textbooks he had previously used. Sandra turned directly to her math textbook and listed the units she found in the table of contents.

Course: Social Studies — 6

Units: I. Learning Skills

II. Tracing the Origins of Primitive Americans

III. Analyzing the Living Patterns of Colonial Americans

IV. Following the Impact of Pioneer Americans upon the Country

Course: Mathematics C

I. Using the Counting Numbers

II. Using Geometry

You have already selected the course and level for a particular content. Now practice breaking that course into units that you would teach over a year's time. You may wish to use the table of contents from several texts as a guide.

Course:_____

Units: I._____

II._____

III._____

IV._____

The third level of content organization involves listing the topics into which you want to divide the units. Each unit should have at least two topics. But again, there is no set number of topics for any unit. Nor do the number of topics have to be the same under the units. One unit may have two topics; another may have nine. These numbers will depend upon how you choose to organize your content. Look once again at your textbook's table of contents. The topics of a unit are really its chapters. For example, in a grammar text the chapters may be: capitalization, punctuation, verbs, and nouns. These will become the topics of the unit. When you write your content, use action verbs to describe what you want the learners to be able to do: **use, solve, analyze, read, write** and **compare** are examples of words that describe what you want the learners to be able to do when they complete the topic or the unit.

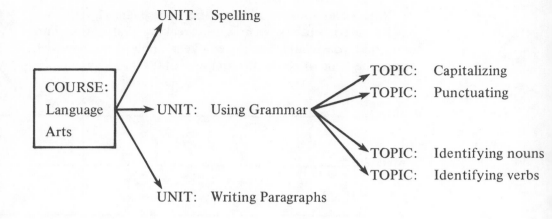

Using Examples of Topics

Don broke his first unit, learning skills, into topics and Sandra did the same to her first mathematics unit.

Course: Course: Social Studies

  Unit: I. Learning Skills

  Topic: A. Exploring the Learning

        B. Understanding and Acting with the Learning

Course: Mathematics C

I. Using Counting Numbers

  A. Understanding Place Values

  B. Adding and Subtracting

Naming Your Topics

Using Don's and Sandra's contents as models, write the topics of each unit you identified in the previous exercise. You should be able to check your content by reversing direction. For example, Don wants his students to explore what is being studied when using the **learning skills** in **Social Studies-6** and Sandra wants the learners to **understand place value** when using the **counting numbers** in **Mathematics C.**

Course:

Unit: I._____

Topics: A. _____

B. _____

C. _____

D. _____

E. _____

58

Unit: II. _____

Topics: A. _____

               B. _____

               C. _____

               D. _____

               E. _____

Unit: III. _____

Topics: A. _____

              B. _____

              C. _____

              D. _____

              E. _____

60

Unit: IV _____

Topics: A. _____

                 B. _____

                 C. _____

                 D. _____

                 E. _____

FINDING THE TASKS

The fourth step in organizing your yearly content, involves finding tasks for each topic. This requires a careful scrutiny of each topic's elements in relation to the unit and the course. Each level is dependent on the one above to make a coherent content. There will be at least two tasks under each topic. It would be advisable to refer again to your textbooks' tables of contents. Under each chapter or topic, you will probably find a list of tasks for that topic. In a language arts course, you may find the following tasks: reviewing action verbs, reviewing auxiliary verbs, determining tenses, and understanding non-standard forms. A word of caution at this point, however: remember that the tasks still have to be broken into at least two daily skills. Therefore, you will want to consider a task as part of your content which takes two days to a week to teach.

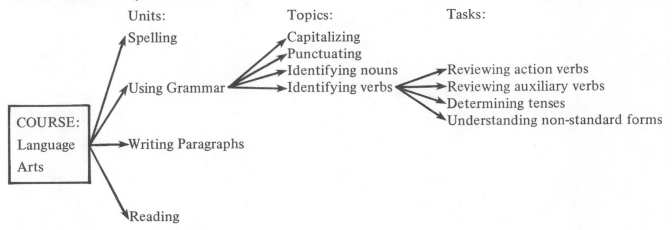

Don and Sandra continued, breaking their first unit and topics into the following tasks:

Course:	Social Studies – 6	
Unit:	I.	Learning Skills
Topics:		A. Exploring the Learning
Tasks:		1. Attending to the learning

2. Responding to the sources of learning

B. Understanding and Acting with the Learning
1. Personalizing the learning

2. Initiating with the learning

Course: Mathematics C

I.   Using Counting Numbers
A.   Understanding Place Value
1.   Ordering the numbers

2.   Using money

B.   Adding and Subtracting
1.   Understanding the concepts

2.   Solving equations

Naming Your Tasks

In this exercise, you will begin to understand how inclusive your content is becoming. As you must write at least two tasks for every topic in the content, you will need a tremendous amount of content detail. As a check step, read your content from the bottom up to see if it makes sense. Make sure that you are using active verbs to describe each task that the learners will do.

Course:_____

Units: I. _____

Topics: A. _____

Tasks: 1. _____

              2. _____

              3. _____

           B. _____

              1. _____

              2. _____

              3. _____

           C. _____

              1. _____

              2. _____

              3. _____

D. _____

   1. _____

   2. _____

   3. _____

II. _____

   A. _____

      1. _____

      2. _____

      3. _____

   B. _____

      1. _____

      2. _____

      3. _____

   C. _____

      1. _____

      2. _____

      3. _____

D. _____

   1. _____

   2. _____

   3. _____

III. _____

   A. _____

     1. _____

     2. _____

     3. _____

   B. _____

     1. _____

     2. _____

     3. _____

   C. _____

     1. _____

     2. _____

     3. _____

D. _____

    1. _____

    2. _____

    3. _____

IV. _____

    A. _____

        1. _____

        2. _____

        3. _____

    B. _____

        1. _____

        2. _____

        3. _____

    C. _____

        1. _____

        2. _____

        3. _____

D. _____

    1. _____

    2. _____

    3. _____

The final step of organizing your content is to determine what the daily skills under each task are. Let's stop to take a closer look at what we mean by "skills." **Skills are what you want your learners to be able to do.** They are things that the learners will learn how to do while they are studying the tasks you have developed. Skills are **measurable.** You can determine how well your learners perform them. Skills are **repeatable.** Your learners have a way to perform the skill again and again. Skills are **observable.** You can watch your learners perform them. Using these three criteria, the following skills could be included under the "action verb" task of the example given earlier: supplying the missing verb, changing the form of the verb and identifying the verb in a simple sentence. To determine what daily skills make up each task, you will have to leave the text's tables of contents and go directly to its inner pages.

If you teach skills, your learners will be able to act with the new learning.

COURSE	UNITS	TOPICS	TASKS	SKILLS
Language Arts	Spelling			
	Using Grammar	Capitalizing Punctuating Identifying nouns	Reviewing action verbs	Supplying the missing verbs Changing the form of the verbs Identifying the verb in a simple sentence
		Identifying verbs	Reviewing auxiliary verbs Determining tenses Understanding non-standard forms	
	Writing Paragraphs			
	Reading			

This breaking down of tasks into skills took Don and Sandra a considerable amount of time. Their main problem was to make sure that they had selected skills. They needed to ask themselves if this learning was what they wanted the student to be able to **do**.

Course: Social Studies — 6

Unit: I. Learning Skills

Topics:
Tasks:
Skills:

A. Exploring the Learning
  1. Attending to the learning
    a. Attending physically
    b. Observing
    c. Listening
  2. Responding to the sources
    a. Responding to content
    b. Responding to meaning

B. Understanding and Acting with the Learning
  1. Personalizing the learning
    a. Personalizing the meaning
    b. Personalizing the problem
  2. Initiating with the learning
    a. Developing the goals
    b. Developing the steps
    c. Taking the steps

Course: Mathematics C

1. Using Counting Numbers

A. Understanding Place Value
  1. Ordering the numbers
    a. Stating "greater than"
    b. Stating "less than"
  2. Using money
    a. Counting pennies
    b. Counting dimes
  3. Naming two, three and four digit numerals
    a. Naming numerals aloud
    b. Writing numerals from words

B. Adding and Subtracting
  1. Understanding the concepts
    a. Combining numbers
    b. Taking away
  2. Solving equations
    a. Find N when $a+N=b$
    b. Find N when $N+a=b$
    c. Find N when $a+b=N$
    d. Find N when $N-a=b$
    e. Find N when $a-N=b$
    f. Find N when $a-b=N$

The last practice exercise in this chapter asks you to list the daily skills included under each task in your content. Remember to ask yourself, as a check step, "Is this what I want my learners to be able to do?" If your course is a year's course, you should have between 120-150 skills.

Course: _____

Units: I. _____

Topics: A. _____

Tasks: 1. _____

Skills: a. _____

             b. _____

             c. _____

         2. _____

             a. _____

             b. _____

             c. _____

         3. _____

             a. _____

             b. _____

             c. _____

B. _____

   1. _____

      a. _____

      b. _____

      c. _____

   2. _____

      a. _____

      b. _____

      c. _____

   3. _____

      a. _____

      b. _____

      c. _____

C. _____

   1. _____

      a. _____

      b. _____

      c. _____

2. _____

   a. _____

   b. _____

   c. _____

3. _____

   a. _____

   b. _____

   c. _____

D. _____

  1. _____

     a. _____

     b. _____

     c. _____

  2. _____

     a. _____

     b. _____

     c. _____

  3. _____

a. _____

b. _____

c. _____

II. _____

   A. _____

     1. _____

       a. _____

       b. _____

       c. _____

     2. _____

       a. _____

       b. _____

       c. _____

     3. _____

       a. _____

       b. _____

       c. _____

   B. _____

1. _____

   a. _____

   b. _____

   c. _____

2. _____

   a. _____

   b. _____

   c. _____

3. _____

   a. _____

   b. _____

   c. _____

C. _____

1. _____

   a. _____

   b. _____

   c. _____

2. _____

a. _____

b. _____

c. _____

3. _____

   a. _____

   b. _____

   c. _____

D. _____

1. _____

   a. _____

   b. _____

   c. _____

2. _____

   a. _____

   b. _____

   c. _____

3. _____

   a. _____

b. _____

c. _____

III. _____

  A. _____

    1. _____

      a. _____

      b. _____

      c. _____

    2. _____

      a. _____

      b. _____

      c. _____

    3. _____

      a. _____

      b. _____

      c. _____

  B. _____

    1. _____

a. _____

b. _____

c. _____

2. _____

a. _____

b. _____

c. _____

3. _____

a. _____

b. _____

c. _____

C. _____

1. _____

a. _____

b. _____

c. _____

2. _____

a. _____

b. _____

c. _____

3. _____

   a. _____

   b. _____

   c. _____

D. _____

1. _____

   a. _____

   b. _____

   c. _____

2. _____

   a. _____

   b. _____

   c. _____

3. _____

   a. _____

   b. _____

c. _____

IV. _____

  A. _____

    1. _____

      a. _____

      b. _____

      c. _____

    2. _____

      a. _____

      b. _____

      c. _____

    3. _____

      a. _____

      b. _____

      c. _____

  B. _____

    1. _____

      a. _____

b. _____

c. _____

2. _____

   a. _____

   b. _____

   c. _____

3. _____

   a. _____

   b. _____

   c. _____

C. _____

1. _____

   a. _____

   b. _____

   c. _____

2. _____

   a. _____

   b. _____

82

c. _____

3. _____

    a. _____

    b. _____

    c. _____

D. _____

1. _____

    a. _____

    b. _____

    c. _____

2. _____

    a. _____

    b. _____

    c. _____

3. _____

    a. _____

    b. _____

    c. _____

"That sure was neat today, huh, Don?" Sandra placed the last of her papers in her brief case. "It's like it finally all came together!"

"You're right, Sandy! Why, I'm leaving today with my content laid out for the next three weeks!"

Sandy nodded her head. "Usually it's a day at a time. If I'm really ambitious, I might lay out the week on Sunday night," she continued. "But can you imagine knowing what you're going to be doing for the whole year?"

Don grinned. "Kind of blows your mind, doesn't it?" He stepped over to the chalkboard and picked up a piece of chalk. "Let me see if I've got this stuff down yet." He wrote "Course" in the middle of the board. "That's what I'm teaching, right?" Sandy perched on the edge of a desk directing her attention to the board. "My wild bunch is going to learn Social Studies-6."

Don turned to the chalkboard and wrote "Unit" three times starting at the top of the board. "Then I plan what units I'll teach my learners during the year."

"Remember that you should use verbs to describe what your learners will have to learn when you teach those units," Sandra chimed in.

"Right you are, Sandy. Got to use verbs," Don muttered to himself. "And you have to have at least two units." Turning to the chalkboard again, Don wrote "Topics" down the next column on the board. "Still use verbs and have at least two topics under each unit?" He turned to Sandra who moved her hand up and down.

"Same for tasks, right?" he questioned as he added tasks to the diagram on the board. "And now the skills — I still need at least two skills under each task."

"It's important to remember that the skills are what you teach in a day." Sandra used her fingers to tick off the three criteria for identifying skills. "Your learners **perform** the skill. You want to be able to **observe** how they perform the skill. And you want the learner to be able to **repeat** the skill."

Don stepped back to survey his diagram. "Five levels, huh? That really cuts through your yearly content doesn't it?" They both smiled and agreed that they were ready for the post-test!

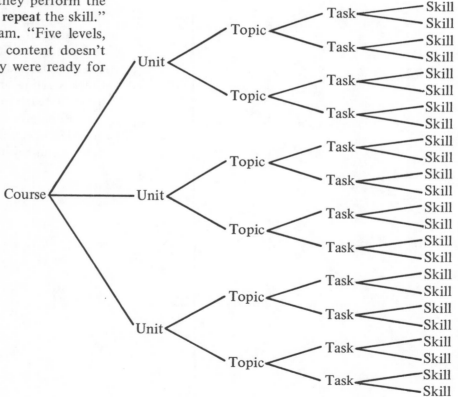

Developing Your Yearly Content

At the beginning of the chapter, you outlined one quarter of a year's content. Now that you have read the chapter and performed the practice exercises, you will want to see how well you have acquired these new content development skills. We will ask you to outline a quarter of a year's content again. You may keep the same content, or choose another to outline.

Sandra chose to re-do the English content she had used in the pre-test. "That way, I can compare the two outlines to see how much more I can include now that I've learned some content development skills."

Look over Sandra's content before you write yours on the pages that follow.

I. Reading

    A. Reading the Short Story

        1. Writing about the plot
           a. Describing the setting
           b. Describing the problem
           c. Describing the main events
        2. Writing about the characters
           a. Describing their appearance
           b. Describing their relationship to the plot
           c. Analyzing their role in the story
           d. Comparing with other characters from previously
               read stories

    B. Doing a Book Report

        1. Writing the report
           a. Listing pertinent information from card catalog
           b. Describing the setting in one sentence
           c. Describing the main characters briefly
           d. Describing the plot briefly
        2. Giving an oral report
           a. Writing main points on a 3" x 5" card
           b. Using correct posture and voice
           c. Speaking in complete sentences from
               one or two word cues

II. Writing

    A. Using Grammar

        1. Identifying parts of speech
           a. Identifying nouns
           b. Identifying verbs

    2.   Writing sentences
        a.   Writing declarative sentences
        b.   Writing interrogative sentences
        c.   Writing exclamatory sentences
    3.   Employing the correct usage
        a.   Using the singular verb forms
        b.   Using the plural verb forms

B.   Using Punctuation

    1.   Writing sentences
        a.   Using the period
        b.   Using the exclamation point
        c.   Using the question mark
        d.   Using the comma
    2.   Writing conversations
        a.   Using italics
        b.   Using the comma
        c.   Capitalizing

C.   Writing a Paragraph

    1.   Using an opening sentence
        a.   Capitalizing
        b.   Punctuating
        c.   Including a subject and a predicate
    2.   Writing the body
        a.   Sequencing sentences
        b.   Answering who, what, when, where, why questions
    3.   Writing the concluding sentence
        a.   Capitalizing
        b.   Punctuating
        c.   Including a subject and a predicate

_____

_____

_____

_____

_____

_____

_____

_____

_____

_____

_____

_____

It was certainly much easier to write up a quarter of a year's content after training. In fact, you may have amazed yourself with how much you had learned in a relatively short time. To complete the post-test measures, rate the following five contents using a five-point scale. The exercise will measure your discrimination ability. Using the scale, rate the contents as follows:

1.0 — Very Ineffective

2.0 — Ineffective

3.0 — Minimally Effective

4.0 — Very Effective

5.0 — Extremely Effective

If you feel a content falls between two levels on the five-point scale, you may rate it as 1.5, 2.5, 3.5, or 4.5. For example, if a content seemed to you to be almost effective but not quite, you would give it a rating of 2.5. You may use a rating more than once.

Your Rating: _____

— Increasing Awareness of Traits of Characters
— Using Comprehensive Strategies
— Textbook Series — Sets A and B
— Storybook Box
— Recognizing Different Forms of Written Language
— Recognizing Story Problem and Solution
— Masters for Independent Study
— Textbook Series — Sets C and D
— Recognizing the Main Idea
— Storybook Box
— Masters for Independent Study
— Content Puzzles, Set 1
— Textbook Series — Sets E and F
— Special Practice Books — Level 2
— Using Organization of Ideas
— Recognizing Alphabetical Order
— Using Alphabetical Order
— Story Puzzles — Set 3
— Textbook Series — Sets G and H
— Masters for Independent Study

92

English — Level I

Reading

Writing

CONTENT B

Your Rating:

Reading the short story

Writing about plot
- Describe setting
- Describe problem
- Describe main events

Writing about characters
- Describe appearance
- Describe relationship to plot
- Analyze role
- Compare with others

Doing a book report

Writing the report
- List catalog information
- Describe setting
- Describe characters
- Describe plot

Giving an oral report
- Writing main points
- Using correct posture and voice
- Speaking in complete sentences

Using grammar

Identifying parts of speech
- Identifying nouns
- Identifying verbs

Writing sentences
- Writing declarative sentences
- Writing interrogative sentences
- Writing exclamatory sentences

Employing correct usage
- Using singular verb form
- Using plural verb form

Using punctuation

Writing sentences
- Using the period and comma
- Using the question mark
- Using italics

Writing conversation
- Using comma
- Capitalizing

Writing a paragraph

Writing an open sentence
- Capitalizing and punctuating
- Writing subject and predicate

Writing the body of a short story

Your Rating:_____

Introductory Earth Sciences

I.   Investigating the Dynamic Earth

    A. Observing the Earth in Space
      1. Viewing from space
      2. Measuring the earth
      3. Proving the earth's rotation
      4. Understanding the seasons

    B. Observing the Earth's Materials
      1. Tracing the origins of rocks
      2. Identifying rocks
      3. Identifying minerals
      4. Investigating mass, volume and density

II.   Investigating the Water Cycle

    A. Observing the Sea
      1. Investigating waves
      2. Investigating currents

    B. Understanding the Water Cycle
      1. Solving what makes the sea salty
      2. Discovering materials that dissolve in sea water

    C. Understanding Evaporation and Condensation
      1. Following the Water Cycle
      2. Investigating evaporation
      3. Investigating melting and boiling
      4. Investigating condensation

III.   Investigating the Rock Cycle

    A. Observing Changes in the Crust
      1. Analyzing weathering
      2. Analyzing how water dissolves substances

    B. Observing Soil
      1. Analyzing how soil develops
      2. Understanding how factors influence the formation of different soils

Your Rating: _____

Mechanical Drawing

1. Using the Language of Drawing
2. Learning to Draw
3. Lettering
4. Drafting Constructions
5. Understanding the Theory of Shape Descriptions
6. Sketching
7. Reading the Graphic Language
8. Inking
9. Reproducing
10. Describing Size
11. Reading Working Drawings
12. Reading Pictorial Drawings
13. Making Technical Illustrations
14. Drafting for Aerospace
15. Drafting for Welding
16. Drafting for Electronics
17. Drafting for Architecture
18. Solving Problems

Your Rating: _____

Mathematics — Book 3

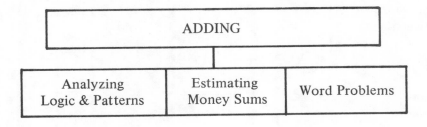

ADDING

| Analyzing Logic & Patterns | Estimating Money Sums | Word Problems |

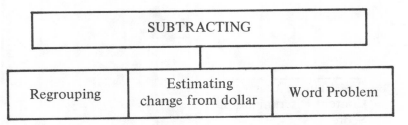

SUBTRACTING

| Regrouping | Estimating change from dollar | Word Problem |

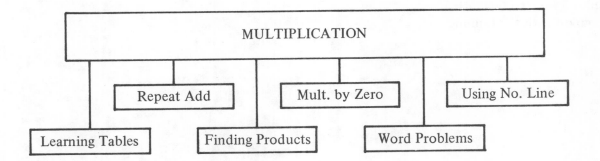

MULTIPLICATION

Repeat Add | Mult. by Zero | Using No. Line

Learning Tables | Finding Products | Word Problems

You are probably quite anxious to see how you did on these post-test assessments. After reading and practicing, you are sure you improved over your pre-training scores at the beginning of this chapter. Well, let's find out how much you improved. To obtain your discrimination score, write down the ratings you made, finding the difference between your score and that of the trained raters. Then add up these differences and divide by five.

Content	Ratings	Your Ratings	Difference
A	1.0	- _____ =	_____
B	5.0	- _____ =	_____
C	4.0	- _____ =	_____
D	2.0	- _____ =	_____
E	3.0	- _____ =	_____

Total _____ = Post-training Yearly
        5   Content Discrimination
                   Score

If your post-training discrimination score is more than .5, you should go back and reread Chapter Two. If your rating was .5 or less, then you are ready to go on with the training.

An explanation of the ratings may help you to review what you have learned about developing the content for a year. The most complete content, with five levels, was English I which rated 5.0. Its effectiveness was due to the fact that it included the course, units, topics, tasks, and skills. Reading this content from right to left, you can understand how the content builds from the day through the year. Almost as effective, was the Earth Science Content, rated 4.0. It failed to receive the highest rating because its tasks were not divided into daily skills. At a rating of 3.0, Content E included only three levels of development: the course, units and topics. The level of detail necessary to understand the mathematics content completely is missing. The mechanical drawing content failed to be effective because it was merely a list of topics under the course title; therefore it received a rating of only 2.0. Content A was extremely ineffective (1.0), because it listed topics and materials indiscriminantly.

Now you understand how the discrimination scores were obtained. You can rate your pre-test and post-test content outlines by simply counting the levels of detail included in your outline. Did you list the course, units, topics, tasks and skills? If so, give yourself a point for each level you included in your outline.

Your Pre-Training Communication Score: _____

Your Post-Training Communication Score: _____

You have just learned that there are five levels to developing content for the year. Beginning with the **course**, you develop the **units** into which the course is divided. The units are broken down into **topics**. Within the topics are **tasks** which the learners need to learn to do. Learners are able to do these tasks because they are broken down into the **skills** the learners must learn. Once your learners have learned the skills of the yearly content, they will be able to do the tasks, topics and units. Then your course will have considerably increased the learners' levels of skills.

Level 1: Course

Level 2: Course and Units

Level 3: Course, Units and Topics

Level 4: Course, Units, Topics and Tasks

Level 5: Course, Units, Topics, Tasks and Skills

Mastering Yearly Content

Once you have mastered yearly content development, you are ready to develop daily content. When an artist begins a canvas, the first step is to sketch the major parts of the composition. This is what the yearly content does. It provides the broad lines which will be detailed later. It would not be appropriate to paint a complete tree on blank canvas before deciding what else is to be included. This is also true of your daily content. If you begin your lesson with the detail of one daily lesson, you may find that the lesson you started with may not fit with the other daily lessons. Your picture will not be complete. As you continue to develop your yearly content, you will find it easier to evaluate textbooks and develop learning materials in your specialty area.

Your yearly content provides the guidelines for your daily content.

"Well, Tracy, I certainly hope you like your new teacher more than you liked Mr. Wexsler last year."

"Oh, yes, **much** more! She's really super! She's already planned out all kinds of neat things we're going to do."

"But I thought you hated the way Mr. Wexsler was always putting you on some kind of schedule last year."

"This is different, Mom! Ms. Jordan says she really wants us to do each new thing **right** before we go on. And listen — I started to worry about what you said, the way Mr. Wexsler was last year with his schedule — and Ms. Jordan understood just what I was feeling. She said I'd feel better once I began to see how much I really could do!"

Effective teachers personalize their year's content — and help individual learners personalize any problems they may have with that content!

SECTION II. ORGANIZING YOUR DAILY CONTENT

3

CHAPTER 3: IDENTIFYING THE SKILLS

Yesterday

"Boy, you sure look grouchy!"

"Oh come on, Helen — just lay off."

"Now is that any way to talk to your big sister? C'mon, what's the matter? Did Mrs. Talkington tell you she didn't like your report or what?"

"No, she thought my report was great. Only — only —"

"Come on, give! What was wrong?"

"Well, she liked it, but I thought it was really dumb! I mean, she didn't teach us anything about how to **give** reports! She just said 'be ready.'"

"So? You were ready, weren't you? Hey, I saw all the stuff you took into class with you!"

"Yeah, sure, I thought I was ready. But — but when it came time to talk — well, I didn't have even a little idea how to do it. I swear, I must've sounded like an idiot up there! All that work — and then I just blabbed for maybe a minute and sat down. It was really dumb, believe me! And the next time she asks us to do reports, I think I'll just get sick and stay home!"

**DEVELOPING THE YEAR'S CONTENT ISN'T ENOUGH!
THE EFFECTIVE TEACHER MUST
DEVELOP AND PERSONALIZE
EACH DAYS' CONTENT AS WELL!**

It seems as if all new units began the same way: what the unit would cover, which chapters in the text should be read, and how to keep your notebook. As a learner yourself in the early grades, you had a chance to tell something you liked about the topic. In the later grades, you heard reports from some of the learners who had already studied the topic. As a learner, however, you probably found that few units provided you with an opportunity to talk about what you expected to get out of the unit. Fewer still provided you with the opportunity to enter the learning from your own frame of reference. Actually, that wouldn't have changed anything anyway. The course was already set. Like any good ship's Captain, the teacher maintained the course. The problem now, as then, is that the ship may make it to port but many of its passengers will not. It is the same with the journey from K to 12. Some learners will make it; others will not.

"I really like Ms. Taylor's class!"

"Yeah? Well you're the only one, then! I don't understand a thing that's going on!"

Without content development skills, all of the class will not learn.

An effective curriculum begins with content development. Content development is simply the way you develop your content. Effective content is developed in a step-by-step manner. Systematic development of content makes it possible for the learners to conquer the learning material involved. In this respect, content development is a precondition of teaching. It is the dimension of teaching which the teacher brings to the learners. Content development is to teaching as attending behavior is to helping. Developing content is a teacher's way of attending to the learners. Just as attending behavior makes it possible for the teacher to get involved in teaching, so content development makes it possible for the learners to get involved in learning. When content has been effectively developed, there is something for the learners to learn. "This is hard — but I like it!" Without effectively developed content, there is nothing for the learners to learn: "Well, 3:00 and another day shot!"

If your content is effective, there will be room for your learners.

Attempting to Develop Steps

You have already had practice planning a year's content. This has given you the large picture of what you will teach. Now it is time to take a closer, more detailed look at the daily skills you will teach. Take the time to select a specific skill from your yearly content. Then write out the content of this daily skill that your learners must know in order to learn that skill.

When Sandra took this pre-test, she selected "describing the setting of a short story" as her skill. The following content describes what she would teach her learners so that they would be able to describe the setting of a short story.

DAILY SKILL: Describing the Setting

A.   Each student will select a favorite short story to read.

B.   Review definition of 'setting.'

C.   Students match the setting from their story to a list of feeling words to show the importance of the setting.

D.   Students will decide if they will describe the setting orally, in writing or by drawing a picture.

E.   They will select the material they need to describe the setting.

F.   Written descriptions of setting can be passed in at the end of the period.

G.   Students will select a time to present their setting descriptions orally.

H.   Drawings of the settings will be hung up around the room

Daily Skill Content: _____

Why is it that pre-tests are so difficult? It's hard to know if you are writing down what you should. There are so many different ways that you could describe what you teach. You should find the discrimination task less difficult though. Given the choice, it is easier to be the critic, than the person who is being criticized. In the next assessment exercise, you will rate five sample daily skills contents. This time, instead of a five-point scale, use a three-point scale as follows:

1.0 — Very Ineffective

2.0 — Ineffective

3.0 — Minimally Effective

If you feel a content falls between two levels on the three-point scale, you may rate it as 1.5 or 2.5. You may also use a rating more than once.

Your Rating:_____

DAILY SKILL: **Understanding the Motives of the Early Colonists**

A.   Introduction and Background

B.   Major Causes
       1. Personal Freedom
       2. Religion
       3. Political
       4. Economic

C.   Effects
       1. Short Range —
       population distribution
       2. Long Range — Economic

D.   Discussion

E.   Summary

Your Rating: _____

Describing the Setting

A. Each student will select a favorite short story to read.

B. Review definition of 'setting.'

C. Students match the setting from their stories with a list of feeling words to show the setting's importance.

D. Students will decide if they will describe the setting orally, in writing or by drawing a picture.

E. They will select the materials they need to describe the setting.

F. Written descriptions of settings may be passed in at the end of the period.

G. Students will select a time to present their setting descriptions orally.

H. Drawings of the setting will be hung up around the room.

Your Rating: _____

Measuring Force When Using an Inclined Plane

   A. Review the weighing of objects on a spring balance.

      1. Place object to be weighed on the hook of the balance.

      2. Hold scale by top so that the object is free of any support.

      3. Read indicator on scale.

      4. Record weight.

   B. Measure force when using an inclined plane.

      1. Weigh object and record.

      2. Set inclined plane at 15°.

      3. Measure force needed to raise weight 8 inches and record.

      4. Set inclined plane at 30°.

      5. Measure force needed to raise weight 8 inches and record.

      6. Set inclined plane at 60°.

      7. Measure force needed to raise weight 8 inches and record.

      8. Make a statement which summarizes your findings about the relationship between the angle of the inclined plane and the force needed to raise the object.

Your Rating: _____

Labeling Isosceles, Equilateral and Scalene Triangles

    A. Hand out mimeographed worksheet containing 12 triangles, 4 of each kind.

    B. Show transparency of types of triangles on overhead.

    C. List 10 things in class that are triangular in shape.

    D. Have students label worksheets.

    E. Have students use rulers to construct their own sample of each triangle.

    F. Show filmstrip on finding the area of a triangle.

Your Rating:_____

Identifying Red, Blue and Yellow Blocks

    A. Ask learners to put blocks of the three colors into three separate groups.

    B. Have several learners hold up a block and call on another student to name the color.

    C. Another learner finds the label of the color and shows the rest of the class.

    D. Paste color labels on chalk tray with a closed box under each.

    E. Learners come up and take turns placing their blocks in the right box.

    F. Have color captains empty boxes on floor to check the colors.

    G. Have each learner write the words "red," "blue" and "yellow" using the correctly colored crayon.

After completing the rating of the five contents, you are probably curious to find out how well you did on the pre-test. In some instances, you were baffled as to the correct rating for these contents. As a first step towards learning to develop your daily content, compare your ratings with those below. Find your pre-training discrimination score by subtracting your ratings from those of the trained raters. Then find the sum of these differences and divide by 5 to obtain your discrimination score.

Daily Skills Content	Ratings		Your Ratings		Difference
A	1.0	-	_____	=	_____
B	2.0	-	_____	=	_____
C	3.0	-	_____	=	_____
D	1.0	-	_____	=	_____
E	2.0	-	_____	=	_____
		Total	=	_____	

$$\frac{}{5} = \underline{}$$

Pre-Training
Daily Content
Discrimination
Score

The lower your discrimination score, the better. A score of .5 or less is considered very good.

But it is not unusual for teachers to receive a score of 1.0 or higher before receiving daily content development training. Such a score shows the need for systematic training. You may be rating a minimally effective content as ineffective. The following pages will help you improve your discrimination of daily skills content.

Let us explain how the pre-training ratings were obtained. That way you can overview the skills you will be learning in the following pages. The key to the completeness of Content C was the inclusion of skill steps which the learners would take to perform the skill. To measure the force needed when using an inclined plane the learners had to do certain steps in a particular order. These steps are clearly listed. Therefore, this content was rated minimally effective at 3.0. Contents B and E received ratings of 2.0 and would be considered ineffective. Describing the setting and identifying red, yellow and blue blocks are both skills. However, the list of steps given in each plan, were really the **teacher's** methodological steps. They listed how the teacher would conduct the class rather than how the learners would be able to perform the skill. Some of the learners may be able to gain insights into how to perform these skills, but the activities do not ensure that all learners will draw the same conclusions from these class activities. Receiving the lowest rating, Contents A and D failed to meet even the first requirement of the daily content. That is, understanding the early colonists' motives and labeling isosceles, equilateral and scalene triangles are not even skills. They involve supportive knowledge that requires the learners to use the skill of recall. And content without skills is very ineffective.

Utilizing this general explanation of the rating system, look back to the daily content that you developed. Rate your content "very ineffective" (1.0) if you did not have a skill for the content. Rate your content "ineffective" (2.0) if it contained a skill but no skill steps that the learners may follow to actually **do** the skill. You may need some help, perhaps from your instructor, to discriminate between method steps and skill steps. Finally, rate your content "minimally effective" (3.0), if you: 1) developed a skill, and 2) developed the skill steps the students would have to perform.

Your Pre-Test Communication Score: _____

Using Feedback for Preparing Steps

Don scowled down at his pre-test scores. "Will you look at that," he said in disgust. "I rated the colors a 3.0 and my communication score is 1.0."

"Oh, don't feel so bad, Don. I don't think anyone did real well. It's kind of demoralizing, isn't it? I mean here we are . . . teachers," Sandra gestured around at the other teachers in the class. "And we can't even write a minimally effective daily content!"

"It's not that I don't know what to teach," continued Don. "But I really fouled up on skills."

"Well you weren't the only one! You know, we teach a lot of things and some are skills and some aren't. But we never really say to ourselves, 'Today I'm teaching a skill' or 'Tomorrow I'm teaching recall.'"

"You're right, Sandy. And that's what we've got to do . . . at least if we're going to get any credit for this workshop."

Before you begin to learn how to write skill steps, you should be sure that you have a skills content. Remember, to be a skill, the learners have to **do** something. Writing a list of words or phrases from memory, or labeling a diagram are not skills in the true sense of the word. There are skills involved: the skill of recall, and the skill of copying. But these are not the kinds of skills that you want the learners to focus on. You want them to learn skills like outlining, multiplication, research and scientific investigation. These are skills with which you can observe and measure your learners' performance. The students should also be able to repeat these skills. So take another look at your daily skills taken from the content you developed in Chapter Two, and ask yourself: "Is this what I want my learners to learn to do?"

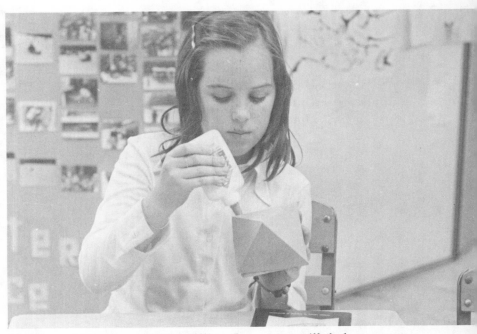

If your content contains skills, then you will help your learners to be more successful in learning.

You will begin developing your daily skills content, by listing the skill steps your learners will follow to perform the skill. The first step will tell the learners where to begin. This step should reflect the learners' abilities. In other words, it should be a step that all the learners can perform successfully.

"Look, Mr. Hahn — I did it!"

"You sure did, Jody — it feels super to get it right, doesn't it?"

The steps that follow should contain all of the instructions the learners need to do the skill correctly. You will need to think carefully about your skill in order to include all the necessary steps.

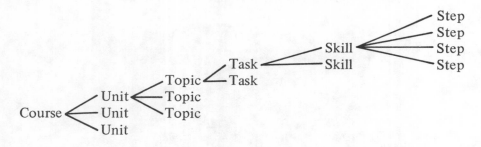

To begin writing the **skill** steps of the daily content, you need a statement of the end result. That is, what your learners will be able to **do** when they complete the **skill** steps. This statement describes the skill objective that you want your learners to achieve. For example, you may want the learners to supply the missing verbs in a sentence. Then the skill statement is: a) Supply the missing verb in a sentence.

COURSE

I. Unit

A. Topic

   1. Task

      a. Skill

It was not difficult for Sandra and Don to return to their yearly content and select a daily skill to use in their practice exercise. Don selected 'attending physically' as his skill, while Sandra chose 'stating **greater than** relationships.'

COURSE; Social Studies 6

I. Learning Skills
    A. Exploring the Learning
        1. Attending to the learning.
           a. Attending physically.

COURSE: Mathematics C

I. Using Counting Numbers
    A. Understanding Place Value
        1. Ordering the numbers
           a. Stating 'greater than' relationships.

Writing the Daily Skill

It is time for you to begin the practice exercise for this chapter. Select a daily skill from the yearly content you developed in Chapter Two. In most cases, you should start with the first skill that appears in your yearly content. Then your steps will not overlap any other areas of study. Write out the skill, so that you know what you want your learners to be able to do.

COURSE: _____

UNIT: _____

TOPIC: _____

TASK: _____

SKILL: _____

There are things you need to think about before you begin writing the **skill** steps. What do your learners need to prepare for these skill steps? What do they need to do while performing the steps, and what will they need to know in order to evaluate their own work? There are discriminations, judgments and decisions that you must think about before starting to write a program of steps. They are things that are automatic to you, in many cases. You have performed the skill so many times that you have mastered it. For the learners, it is a different story. You must tell them all they need to know so they can be successful in performing the skill. To do that you must answer the questions about who, what, when, where, why and how.

"How do we start this, anyway?"

"You're confused because you don't know what you should do first. That's certainly understandable. All right, your first step is . . ."

If you answer the basic questions, your learners will be successful in performing the skill.

While the specific questions may vary from skill to skill, the basic interrogatives will help you to identify many "think" questions.

Who?	Who will do it?
Why?	Why is this skill important?
What?	What is to be done? What is needed to do it?
Where?	Where should it be done?
When?	When should it be done? When should each piece be used?
How?	How do you do the skill? How do you know you've done it right?

As the teacher of the skill, there are two things you must do. First, list all the questions that relate to using the particular skill you have selected. Second, answer these questions. Your answers will enable you to write the skill steps. This process is very much like taking out an intellectual insurance policy; it helps you write a **complete** skill step program. If you leave holes in your program, then one of your learners may fall through. The answers to your "think" questions will become the steps necessary to perform the skill.

Before attending physically, there are many things that Don must think about in order to develop a Learning Skills content.

These "think" questions may be illustrated with the basic interrogatives as follows:

SKILL: I want the learners to be able to **attend physically** (last step).

In order to write the learners' program of **attending physically**, I must ask the folowing questions.

1. With **whom** are the learners to perform the skill?
2. **What** are they going to do with the other person?
3. **When** and **where** can the learners perform the skill?
4. **Why** are they going to perform the skill?
5. **How** are they going to perform the skill?
6. How will they know they are doing it right?

In order to write the learners' program of attending physically, I must answer the above questions.

1. (Who) The learners are going to perform the skill with **me** and their learning **materials**.
2. (What) They are going to pay attention.
3. (When and Where) The learners are going to attend **in my class** while they are **in the room**.
4. (Why) They are going to attend so that they can **prepare themselves for learning**.
5. (How) They are going to **square**, **lean** and **make eye contact**.
6. They will know they are doing it right if they are facing the source of learning, leaning toward it and can see it.

Now take the skill you have already selected. This can be the skill you have developed throughout this chapter. List all the questions you must answer before you do this skill. Then answer these "think" questions. Make certain that all of the questions you ask are directly related to the skill to be performed. Be sure that you include a way for the learners to evaluate their own work. This usually becomes a "think step" in the learner's program.

YOUR MODEL SKILLS PROGRAM

Preparing **Before Think** Steps

SKILL: I want the learners to be able to _____

_____

In order for the learners to _____
I must ask the "think" questions:

1. _____

2. _____

3. _____

4. _____

5. _____

In order for the learners to _____
I must answer the "think" questions:

1. _____

2. _____

3. _____

4. _____

5. _____

These answers will help you get ready to write the skill steps.

Writing the first step of the program requires you to use the "think" questions and answers you just developed. They have helped you think about the new skill. You must now determine what is the very first thing your learners must do to reach the last step. If you want the learners to supply the missing verb in a sentence, their first step would be to read the sentence. It is critical that your learners succeed in doing the first step, if they are ever to reach the last. If the learners can complete the first step successfully, they will be able to attempt the next step in your daily program.

COURSE

I.   Unit
   A.   Topic
      1.   Task
         a.   Skill
            1)   Step

Don and Sandra used their "think" questions to help them choose their first skill steps, in particular the "how" think questions. Don wanted his learners to attend to him and the learning materials. Therefore, he included that information in the first step. Sandra used the "think" questions to come up with the simplest step her learners could do: graphing the numbers on a number line.

COURSE: Social Studies 6

I. Learning Skills

    A. Exploring the Learning
      1. Attending to the learning
        a. Attending physically
          1) Posture self squarely in relation to teacher and learning materials

COURSE: Mathematics C

I. Using Counting Numbers

    A. Understanding Place Value
      1. Ordering the numbers
        a. Stating "greater than" relationship
          1) Draw number line to include two numbers being compared

Using the "think" questions and answers you have developed, write the very first thing you would want your learners to do in performing the skill. Make sure that it is the simplest step your learners can take successfully.

COURSE: _____

UNIT: _____

TOPIC: _____

TASK: _____

SKILL: _____

STEP 1: _____

Once you have written the first **skill** step, you can continue to write the remaining skill steps. These steps will bring your learners from the first step to the last. They will culminate in the learners' being able to perform the skill. For example, after reading a sentence missing a verb, ask yourself: "What do the learners have to do to fill in the correct missing verb?" Thinking through what you would do, you may write the following steps: 1) read the sentence; 2) place the first verb in your list in the blank and reread the sentence; 3) ask yourself if the sentence makes sense, 4) insert the next word into the sentence; 5) ask yourself if the sentence makes sense with that word in it; 6) continue testing all the listed words. It is important to include all the steps that your learners need in order to complete the skill. A reaction like "I did what you said but it still doesn't come out right," means that you have failed to personalize the development of steps in terms of the learners' frames of reference. Test the skill steps by doing the skill yourself, following the steps you have written.

COURSE

I. UNIT

  A. Topic

    1. Task

      a. Skill
        1) Step
        2) Step
        3) Step
        4) Step
        5) Step

Sandra and Don spent some time developing their middle skill steps. They tested each other's steps by following them to see if that was actually what they did when they performed the skill. Sandra found that Don had left a step out of his program. "It's fine to have the kids square, lean and make eye contact, Don. But you know that their biggest problem is sitting still."

"You've got a point there, Sandy," answered Don. "They could square, lean and make eye contact while they jiggled, chewed and twitched. I've got to put another step in my program about distractions."

Study both Don's and Sandra's programs to see if you think they are complete.

COURSE: Social Studies 6

I. Learning Skills

   A. Exploring the Learning
      1. Attending to the learning
         a. Attending physically
            1) Posture self squarely in relation to teacher and learning materials.
            2) Lean forward.
            3) Stop distracting motions.
            4) Make eye contact with teacher or learning materials.

COURSE: Mathematics C

I. Using Counting Numbers

   A. Understanding Place Value
      1. Ordering the numbers
         a. Stating "greater than" relationships
            1) Draw number line to include two numbers being compared.
            2) Find number farthest to the right.
            3) Write that number, then ' > ' symbol and finally, the number to the left.
            4) Read over what you have written to yourself.

As you write the remaining steps of your daily content, you will ask yourself if they adequately describe what your learners must do to complete the skill. Many learners fail because they cannot supply the steps that are missing: "I thought I had it, but I goofed!" The only reason that some succeed, is that they are able to supply these steps: "Oh boy, it really works!"

You can expedite the learning process when you teach your learners all the steps they need to learn. These steps should be small enough for the learners to follow them easily. Remember to check to see if you can perform the skill successfully by following the steps you have written.

COURSE: _____

UNIT: _____

TOPIC: _____

TASK: _____

SKILL: _____

STEPS: _____

_____

_____

_____

_____

Don swung around in his seat. "This stuff is sure a lot of work! But once I get it down, it's going to be powerful!"

"You're right, Don," responded Sandra. "I'm still cloudy on some of these steps, though. Can you help me?"

"Sure, Sandy! Let's start at the beginning, but it's really the end. Well . . . what I mean is that you start by writing the daily skill first."

Sandy nodded her head, "Uh huh."

"Next come the "think" questions. They help you get ready to write the skill steps."

"Oh," Sandy squinted up toward the ceiling, "That's those questions, right? Who, what, when, where, why and how, right? Once I've answered the "think" questions I can write my first skill step."

"You've got it, Sandy," responded Don. "And that first step has to be the very first one your learners do to perform the skill. Then you can go ahead and write the remaining steps."

"It's beginning to sink in, Don. Now I'm ready for that post-test."

Sandy went to the chalkboard. "I've got an idea. Why can't I review what we've just learned by writing the skill steps of writing skill steps?" Don looked puzzled. "I mean OUR skill steps to develop content, Don," she replied. "Like this." And she wrote the following steps on the chalkboard.

LAST STEP

SKILL STEPS

Write
Skill
Steps

Write
Remaining
Steps

Write the
First Skill
Step

Answer
Think
Questions

FIRST STEP

Ask
Think
Questions

Write the
Daily Skill
as Last Step

Once Don and Sandy saw their own skills programs laid out in steps, they went back to their yearly content. Taking a unit of skills they had written, they wrote the skill steps for each skill in the unit. You will want to take the time now to reaffirm your new learning. Continue to develop the skill steps for each of your skills that are contained in your first unit. Remember to check your programs of skill steps by following them to perform the skill yourself.

If your content contains all the skill steps, then the learners will be able to perform the skill.

132 POST-TRAINING SKILLS STEP ASSESSMENT

You have spent hours practicing your new content development skills. Breaking so many skills into steps is an extremely disciplined activity. But you should realize that you have learned a tremendous amount about your content area things you had forgotten that you knew. This learning will make you that much more successful in your teaching. In addition, you should have little trouble demonstrating your skill growth in the communications post-test. Take the time now to select a skill and write the skill steps that your learners must follow to perform the skill. Use the "think" questions and answers to help you write the completed steps.

SKILL: _____

Skill Steps: _____

_____

_____

_____

_____

_____

_____

_____

_____

_____

_____

_____

Of course, writing out the skill steps must have been an easier task for you after all the practice you have had. You should feel more comfortable about rating the daily skills content in the following discrimination test. Again, you will use a three-point scale to rate the effectiveness of the following contents.

1.0 — Very Ineffective

2.0 — Ineffective

3.0 — Minimally Effective

If you judge a content as falling between two levels, you may split the difference between the two ratings, using 1.5 or 2.5. In addition, you may use a rating more than once.

Your Rating: _____

Printing the Letters "b" and "d"

    A. To make a "b"
1. Place your pencil on the top line.
2. Draw a straight, vertical line to the bottom line.
3. Place your pencil in the middle of the vertical line.
4. Draw a half-circle to the right of the vertical line so that it rests on the bottom line.

    B. To make a "d"
1. Place your pencil on the top line.
2. Draw a straight, vertical line to the bottom line.
3. Place your pencil in the middle of the vertical line.
4. Draw a half-circle or "C" to the left of the vertical line so that it rests on the bottom line.

Your Rating:_____

Developing New Systems for Measurement

    A. Discuss importance of measurement.
        1. Answer how you use it.
        2. Answer how your parents use it.

    B. Living on Mars, you would have different units because you had never heard of a pound or an inch.
        1. How would you measure how much things weigh on Mars?
        2. How would you measure how long things were on Mars?

    C. Learners will select three things to measure (length and weight).
        1. Use units they invented.
        2. Explain their system to the rest of the class.

Your Rating:————————————————————

Spelling — Unit III

    A. The learners will be able to spell correctly 8 out of 10 words listed on page 42.
        1. Read the story.
        2. Underline the new words in the story.
        3. Write the words 3 times each.
        4. Fill in the exercise on page 43.
        5. Quiz your neighbor orally to prepare for mastery test on Friday.

Your Rating:_____

Punctuating Declarative and Interrogative Sentences

1. Half of the class will be assigned to find two sentences that constitute a statement in their social studies books.
2. The other half of the class will find two sentences that ask a question in their science books.
3. Class takes turns preparing transparencies, passing them around the room, and writing their sentences.
4. Punctuation marks are not included on the transparencies.
5. Teacher numbers the sentences.
6. Class practices, choosing either a period or a question mark to punctuate the end of the sentence.
7. Students exchange papers to correct and receive immediate feedback.

Your Rating: _____

Carrying a Microscope

1. With the right hand, grasp the arm of the microscope.
2. Lift the microscope straight up.
3. Support the base of the microscope with your left hand at the same time.
4. Walk to your lab station and gently place the microscope on the lab table.

Checking Out Your Content Discriminations

Again, the trained raters' ratings are listed below. You may determine the discrimination score by obtaining your absolute deviations, adding them and dividing the total by 5. The resulting number is your content discrimination score.

Daily Content	Ratings	Your Ratings		Difference
A	3.0	- _____	=	_____
B	2.0	- _____	=	_____
C	1.0	- _____	=	_____
D	2.0	- _____	=	_____
E	3.0	- _____	=	_____
		TOTAL =		

$$\frac{\qquad}{5} = \frac{\qquad}{\text{Post-Training Daily Content Discrimination Score}}$$

As you read the following explanation of the ratings, you will see specific applications of what you have learned about skill steps. Perhaps you had a pretty good idea which daily contents were most effective. And yet you could not actually explain in words why one content was effective and the other ineffective. This is why the following explanation of the ratings can add to what you already know.

The two effective skills contents were contents A and E. They rated at 3.0. Printing "b" and "d" are skills and the skill steps necessary to perform them are included in the content. The content for the skill of carrying a microscope is also effective as .it contains the steps the learners must do to perform this skill. Contents B and D are ineffective (2.0) because they confuse the teacher's methods with the content: the teacher hopes that the learners will intuit the new skills, by just doing a list of learning activities. And many learners may be able to do this. However, it is not an efficient or dependable method for all the learners. To be able to punctuate declarative and interrogative sentences, the learners need content in the form of skill steps as well as learning activities. With these, the teacher can be successful with not just a few learners but with **all** the learners. For its rating of 1.0, Content C was extremely ineffective because the spelling of a list of words from rote is not considered a skill. In order for the spelling to be considered a skill, the content must include some sort of rules which the learners can follow to do the skill correctly.

At this point, you should evaluate your communication score for daily content development. Examine the skill and skill steps you developed for the post-test exercise. If your daily content is not a skill, rate it as 1.0, or 'very ineffective.' If it is a skill, but you have not developed step-by-step instructions for your learners to follow to perform the skill, then rate your content at 2.0. In order to receive an 'effective' rating of 3.0, your content should include the skill steps for the skill you want the learners to be able to do.

Your Pre-Training Communication Score: _____

Your Post-Training Communication Score: _____

Understanding Skill Steps

Having completed the post-training assessment, you have a better understanding of a **skills content**. These practice exercises began by having you focus on what you want the learners to be able to **do**. By asking the **think** questions and answering them, you have become more familiar with the skill in relation to the learners. The answer to the **think** questions have prepared you to write the **learners' skill steps**. When you write the content using skill steps, you are listing what your learners will do to perform a skill, rather than how you will teach it.

Level 1.0: Non-Skills Content

Level 2.0: Skills

Level 3.0: Skills and Skill Steps

Mastering Skill Steps

You have filled in a basic sketch of your yearly content by writing the learner's skill steps. These steps add more detail to your outline so that you know what you must teach. And as you write these steps, you are readied for the next level of content detail. At this moment, your content is like a picture that looks good from a distance. Yet when you step closer to the canvas you notice a lack of detail. The picture appears flat and incomplete. To complete your daily content you need to define the supportive knowledge your learners need to **know** in order to **do** the skill steps. That is, you will write the facts, concepts and principles of your daily content. Continuing to learn content development skills will enable you to make good decisions about what books and materials to use in your classroom. These skills can be used to produce curriculum and related learning materials.

When you teach your learners the skill steps, they can perform the skill.

"How come you're flying so high? I thought today was the day for your big spring report for Ms. Talkington."

"Yeah, so?"

"Well, last fall you said you'd never do another report for her."

"That just shows how much **you** know! Maybe last fall wasn't so hot. But Ms. Talkington's been doing a lot of new stuff with us this spring."

"Oh Yeah? Like what, for instance?"

"Like teaching us how to give good reports, for one! Listen, we spent yesterday and the day before practicing the things anyone needs to do to give an oral report in front of a bunch of other people. Like how to stand and how to use notes — stuff like that! It's a whole lot different than before. When I get up to give my report in class today, I'm really going to know what I'm doing."

"My little brother — star of his 6th grade Social Studies class! C'n I get your autograph?"

"How'd you like a punch in the nose instead?"

"Oh, Nick, I'm just kidding. You know that! Listen, I'm really glad you feel better about giving this report."

"Yeah? Well that makes you maybe half as glad as I am. You know, I'm really beginning to look forward to my class with Ms. Talkington!"

Content development skills help learners see each day's class as an opportunity to grow and excel.

CHAPTER 4: IDENTIFYING THE SUPPORTIVE KNOWLEDGE

Yesterday

"Mandy — must you gulp your food like that? Anyone'd think we never feed you!"

"Huh? Oh — sorry, Dad, but I gotta get over to Larissa's to work on our science homework."

"Yes? Well, what is your homework? It must be pretty complicated if you both need to work on it."

"Complicated? Yeah, I guess . . . We're making a light box."

"A what?"

"A light box! See, we made this box out of some pine boards. And we made a screen for the front out of some old dress lining material. Now we've got to stick some Christmas lights we've got up against the back wall of the box and hang stuff between the lights and the cover. Then we can turn it on, and turn some music on, and it'll look neat!"

"I see — but how is that a science project?"

"Oh, we've been working on light sources and stuff."

"So what will your light box demonstrate?"

"Huh? Oh, I dunno — it'll just look neat, that's all. When the project's over, Larissa and I are going to take turns keeping it. I want it on my bookshelf right next to the radio!"

"Fine, fine — but what are you **learning**?"

"Learning? Oh — well — I guess we're learning how to put together a light box. Anyway, who cares?"

**CONTENT MUST DELIVER MORE THAN
THE ABILITY TO DO SOMETHING — IT
MUST DELIVER AN UNDERSTANDING OF
WHAT'S BEING DONE!**

You have completed many levels of detail in your content development. At this point you have laid out a year's content. It does not seem possible that there could be more for you to teach. But what about all those **names** and **ideas** that your learners will need to know?

Perhaps you have known learners who could do a lot of things. And yet, when it came time to communicate, they were not able to express themselves. This was so because they did not have an adequate base of **supportive knowledge**. "Pass me the thing over there", or, "The thing goes kinda like this," are common forms of expression for learners who are deficient in supportive knowledge. In fact, they should be able to say "Pass me the plastic protractor on John's desk" or "The wheel turns in a clockwise direction." Yes! It is important for your learners to be able to communicate these skills to others.

When the learners know the supportive knowledge, they can communicate more fully.

You have been a learner in many classrooms which emphasize learning supportive knowledge. Memorizing lists, copying diagrams and answering questions were the learning tasks in these classes. Sometimes it was difficult to learn these new facts and concepts. You probably remembered them until the test was completed and then promptly forgot them. And herein lies the problem. While it is important for the learners to acquire supportive knowledge, they must also achieve a balance between knowing and doing. For this reason, you should teach and personalize the supportive knowledge of a skill in relation to performing the skill.

"So the round things we grow our cultures in are called Petri dishes?"

"That's right. Doesn't it feel better when you can give something a definite name?"

If you teach only supportive knowledge, your learners will become bored.

Attempting to Identify the Supportive Knowledge

You have already had considerable practice writing the content you will teach during the year. Yet you know there is more to your content than just skills and skill steps. Take the time now to write the complete content you would teach your learners in one class lesson. You may select any content for this exercise. Before you begin, you may want to take a look at Sandra's pre-test.

"Let me see," said Sandra to herself. "The content of a day's lesson . . . hum. Well, I know enough to include the skill and the skill steps." She tapped her pencil nervously on the desk and started to write. "I'll select a math lesson this time."

    I. Using Counting Numbers

      A. Understanding Place Value

         1. Ordering the numbers

            a. Using "greater than"

               1) Draw a number line to include the two numbers being compared

                    (number line - ⟵—┼┼┼┼┼—⟶)

                            0 1 2 3 4

               2) Find number farthest to the right.

               3) Write that number, then '>' and finally the number to the left:

                    (> = is greater than)

               4) Read what you have written to yourself to check work.

               5) State "greater than" relationship.

Skill: _____

As part of your self-assessment, you need to evaluate how well you can discriminate the supportive knowledge in your content. Rating the following five contents will give you this opportunity.

You will use a five-point scale where you rate the contents:

1.0 — Very Ineffective

2.0 — Ineffective

3.0 — Minimally Effective

4.0 — Very Effective

5.0 — Extremely Effective

Again, if you feel a content falls between two levels on the five-point scale, you may split the gap and rate it as 1.5, 2.5, 3.5 or 4.5. For example, if a content seems to you to be between "minimally effective" and "very effective," you would give it a 3.5. You may use a rating more than once.

Your Rating: _____

Skill: Describing the setting of a short story in one sentence. (If you are describing the setting, then you will tell where and when the story takes place).

1.   Read the Short-Story
                (Short Story)

2.   Answer the question: "Where does the story take place?"
         Where — In what country? In an urban (city), suburban (around city), rural (farms) or wilderness area (few people)?

3.   Answer the question: "When does the story take place?"
         When — Past? (before the present)
                   Present? (now)
                   Future? (after the present)

4.   Write: The story takes place **(where)** in **(when)**.

Your Rating:———————————————————

Skill: Measuring force when using an inclined plane

1.   Weigh object and record.
2.   Set inclined plane at 15°.
3.   Measure force needed to raise weight 8 inches and record.
4.   Set inclined plane at 30°.
5.   Measure force needed to raise weight 8 inches and record.
6.   Set inclined plane at 60°.
7.   Measure force needed to raise weight 8 inches and record.
8.   Make a statement which summarizes relationship between angle of the inclined plane, and the force needed to raise the object (angle — $<$).

Your Rating: _____

Skill: Bisecting a line segment with a compass.
1.   (If you bisect a line, you divide it into 2 equal parts and two equal segments.)

2.   Line segment — part of line.
3.   Compass — instrument to draw circle of various sizes.
4.   Make arcs above and below the segment like this: 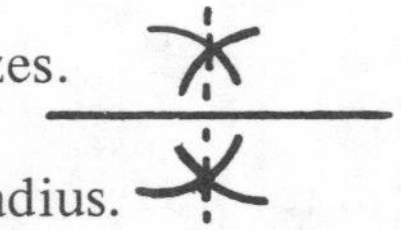
5.   Arcs — part of a circle. These arcs have the same radius.
6.   Radius — the distance from the center of the circle to point on the outside of the circle.

Your Rating:_____

Skill: Carrying a microscope

1.   With right hand grasp the arm of the microscope
              arm — connects barrel to base

                    arm

              grasp — hold firmly.

2.   Lift the microscope straight up.

      straight up

3.   Support the base of the microscope in the palm of your left hand.

Your Rating:_____

Skill: Labeling the parts of a business letter
       (When these parts are all included, they tell the receiver who, what, when, where
       and why: all the information which he or she needs to know).

1.   Date — top right-hand corner.
2.   Inside address — to whom you are writing and the person's address.
3.   Salutation — greeting, usually "Dear_____:".
4.   Body — where you say what needs to be said.
5.   Closing — several words such as "Yours truly,".
6.   Signature - your name.

Obtaining Your Pre-Training Discrimination Score

Now you are ready to obtain your pre-test score for developing the supportive knowledge of your content. Even though you had considerable practice in writing skill steps, you probably found that it was not an easy task to evaluate the effectiveness of the five contents. Compare your ratings with those listed below. Subtract the difference between your ratings and those of trained raters. Add these differences, dividing by 5 to obtain your discrimination score.

Skill Content	Ratings		Your Ratings		Difference
A	5.0	-	_____	=	_____
B	1.0	-	_____	=	_____
C	4.0	-	_____	=	_____
D	2.0	-	_____	=	_____
E	3.0	-	_____	=	_____
		Total	=	_____ / 5	= _____

Pre-Training Knowledge
Discrimination Score

Receiving an explanation of the discrimination scores helps you overview the new skills you are about to learn. Content A, describing the setting of a short story, received a very effective rating of 5.0. First, it includes the labels or facts the learners will need to perform the steps. Those facts are **short story**, **urban**, **suburban**, **rural**, **wilderness**, **past**, **present** and **future**. Next, the content includes the concepts or ideas the learners would need to do the steps. "Where" and "When" are concepts that need to be defined when teaching this skill. This content also contains a principle of describing the setting. "If you are describing the setting, then you will tell where and when the story takes place." Facts, concepts and principles define supportive knowledge. Content A is a skill and also includes the skill steps necessary to do the skill.

Bisecting a line segment is a skill but the steps of performing that skill are not well defined. Even though Content C contains the supportive knowledge, it rated 4.0 because it lacks the skill steps. Content E rated 3.0 because it consisted of only supportive knowledge. Labeling the parts of a business letter is not a skill, but writing correct business letters would be. While carrying a microscope is a skill, Content D contains the steps of carrying a microscope without giving a principle of the skills. Therefore, it rated as 2.0. Content B rated 1.0 because only a few facts were defined for the learners; this Content did not contain all the supportive knowledge they would need to learn the skill.

Using Feedback for Supportive Knowledge

Sandra was chagrined to find that her daily content rated 1.0 or "very ineffective." "After all this time, you'd think I'd learn," she said with exasperation. "I had the skill and steps down perfectly, but I really missed the boat on those concepts and principles."

"I think we all did, Sandra," Don joined in. "What the heck! I'm not even sure I understand the concept of 'concept.'"

Sandra reacted with a grimace. "I think you've got a point, Don. Let's get busy and learn what this stuff means."

You have taken your content and broken it down into more detail starting with the course that you teach. As you develop the content, you move from the units through successive levels. Once you develop the skills level of the content, you are focusing on the daily content to be taught. Your learners should learn the principle of what the skill does: "How come this works like this?" They will need to learn certain facts and concepts that are included in the skill steps: "What's this part called? What's it do?" We group facts, concepts and principles as the supportive knowledge of the skill.

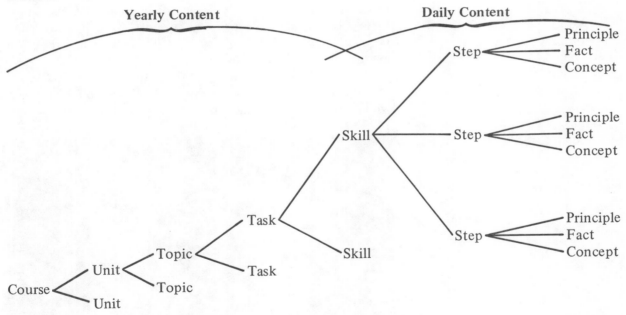

Again, follow Don and Sandra as they learn to write the facts, concepts and principles of their skills content. Use their content as a sample to list the facts, concepts and principles of one of your skills in the practice exercises. Select one skill for these exercises from your yearly content. Then write the skill steps the learners must take to do this skill. Later you will practice this content development on other skills.

Your learners need to know facts so that you can tell and show them about the new learning.

IDENTIFYING THE FACTS

The first thing that you want to do is to identify the **facts** related to the skills you are teaching. The **facts** are the simplest things to learn about the skill. **Facts are the names or labels we attach to things to identify them**. They are nouns that answer the question "What is it?" In relation to a skill, facts are the things involved in performing its steps. Most often, facts are the names of people, places and things. As you may already know, teaching facts by themselves is dangerous because there is so little you can do with them. Sure, you communicate about things by just using their names. They are particularly important to know for tests. But in the final analysis, you cannot **implement** facts. Thus, facts are considered a primary support level of knowledge because they enable learners to talk about what they are learning to do.

"We're supposed to pick out the active verbs, right?"

"That's right, Penny — I'm glad to see you know just where you're going — and I bet you're glad, too!"

Facts Are the First Level of Knowledge

It will probably be no problem for you to identify the facts of your specialty area because these are what you learned most in school. Facts are the things you stayed up late the night before the test trying to memorize. Yet now you may have forgotten many of them. Facts are the things that those prepared dittoed tests and worksheets ask your learners. The final outcome — eventual forgetfulness — will be the same for them as for you unless you decide to teach the **relevant** supportive facts. Ask yourself: "Do my learners need to know this fact to implement this skill?" and "Will knowing this fact help them to perform this skill better?" Teaching the facts which are only related to the performance of skills will help you keep your content relevant. It is when you try to teach facts unrelated to the skills that your program loses its potency.

COURSE

I. Unit
  A. Topic
    1. Task
      a. Skill
        1) Step
          a) Facts

For example, Don's learners must know what "eye contact" is before they can make eye contact with another person. Indeed, before they can posture their bodies in relation to the learning materials, they must know what **learning materials** are. As can readily be seen, Don may assume that his learners already know many of the facts of his learning program. Facts are perhaps the least important ingredient. Here, Don determines the necessary facts that his learners need to learn to perform the skill step of his model skills program. In a similar way, you will determine the facts that are necessary for your learners to understand the skill steps of your content.

161 COURSE: Social Studies – 6

I. Learning Skills

   A. Exploring the Learning

      1. Attending to the learning

         a. Attending physically

            1) Posture squarely in relation to teacher or learning materials.

               a) Facts: teacher, learning materials

            2) Lean forward.

               a) Facts: none

            3) Stop distracting motions.

               a) Facts: distracting motions

            4) Make eye contact with teacher or look at materials.

               a) Facts: eye contact

COURSE: Mathematics C

I. Using Counting Numbers

  A. Understanding Place Value

    1. Ordering the numbers

      a. Stating "greater than" relationships

        1) Draw number line to include the two numbers being compared.

          a) Facts: number line, number

        2) Find number farthest to the right.

          a) Facts: none

        3) Write that greater number, then '>' symbol and finally number to left or smaller.

          a) Facts: symbol: '>'

        4) Read what you have written to yourself.

          a) Facts: none

163 Developing the Necessary Facts

Now you can include the facts your learners will need for each skill step in the content that you have chosen to develop. Include only the names of people, places, or things that are involved in performing the skill steps. That way you keep your content relevant.

1. Skill: _____

What you know **about** a fact is called a **concept**. Concepts describe the nature or characteristics of things. Therefore, adjectives and adverbs are concepts. Concepts describe what something does. Thus, verbs are also concepts. Concepts are what we know about something. This is why our levels of knowledge involve all we know about something — even how to implement it. Your concept of "sitting" enables you to recognize the object you sit on as a chair, even if it doesn't have legs. A child's concept of "hot" may be identical to the object, or fact — "stove." Later, the child will attach additional facts and concepts to the word "hot" such as "match," "friction," and "molecular motion," as his or her knowledge of "hotness" expands.

"I know another way to get something hot! Make it go around and rub against something else — like the tires on my Mom's car!"

"Great Sheila! It's really fun to discover new ways of doing something, isn't it?"

Your learners need to know concepts so that they can understand how to perform the skill steps.

What can your learners do with concepts? If facts are the names of things, then your learners may, at some point, only know one fact about something. Conceptual learning enables the learners to organize what they know. They can name what they know and can tell you one or more things about what they know. But in the final analysis, they cannot **implement** a concept any more than they can implement a fact. Concepts can only be recalled.

"What is that?"

"A butterfly." (Fact)

"Why?"

"Because it has large (concept), colored (concept) wings (fact)."

"Because it is pretty (concept)."

"Right (concept). And I bet you feel pretty smart because you knew all those answers!" (Personalizing the content.)

COURSE

I.   Unit

A. Topic

   1. Task

    a. Skill

     1) Step

      a) Facts

      b) Concepts

Using a Model for Developing the Necessary Concepts in a Skills Content

To implement the skill of attending, as described in Don's Learning Skills curriculum, it is necessary for his learners to understand certain concepts before they can implement any skill steps. Before his learners can posture themselves in relation to Don, they must understand the concepts of posturing and squaring. Before they can lean forward in relation to Don, they must understand the concepts of leaning and forward. Before they can make eye contact with Don, they must understand the concept of eye contact. In a similar way, concepts lay the groundwork for implementing the skill steps. Here Don simply determines the concepts necessary to perform the skill steps of his content.

I. Learning Skills

   A. Exploring the Learning

      1. Attending to the Learning

         a. Attending Physically

           1) Posture squarely in relation to teacher or learning materials.
              a) Facts: teacher, learning materials
              b) Concepts: posture, squarely
           2) Lean forward.
              a) Facts: none
              b) Concepts: lean, forward
           3) Stop distracting motions.
              a) Facts: distracting motions
              b) Concepts: stop
           4) Make eye contact with teacher or materials.
              a) Facts: eye contact
              b) Concepts: none

167 COURSE: Mathematics C

I. Using Counting Numbers

   A. Understanding Place Value

      1. Order the numbers

         a. Stating "greater than" relationships

            1) Draw number line to include the two numbers that are being compared.

                a) Facts: number line, number

                b) Concepts: draw, compared

            2) Find number farthest to the right.

                a) Facts: none

                b) Concepts: find, farthest, right

            3) Write that greater number, then '>' symbol and finally, the number to the left on number line.

                a) Facts: symbol, '>'

                b) Concepts: write, left, greater, smaller

            4) Read what you have written to yourself.

                a) Facts: none

                b) Concepts: read

Now you will need to identify the concepts in your own model skills program. Take each step of your skills content and identify all the concepts in that step. To check your discriminations, ask yourself if the concepts you have selected are verbs, adjectives or adverbs.

1. Skill:_____

There are many principles related to every skill you teach. One kind of principle describes **why** or **how** something works the way it does. This principle helps the learner to understand how his or her world works. It's the answer to the 4 year-old's, "Why?" "When the big hand goes around one time, one hour has passed." "If you use a ruler to steady the pencil, the line will be straighter." "If you increase the angle of an inclined plane, then the effort needed to push the block will also increase." Each of these principles deals with the idea of "cause and effect." They explain a cause-and-effect relationship for some aspect of the skill. Note that the principle deals only with the content and not with its relationship to the learner.

"So if I write a good topic sentence for my paragraph, then I'll be identifying the main idea of the paragraph, so that I can make every other sentence relate to that one!"

"Yes Nancy, and you feel more sure of yourself when you have a way to check your topic sentences!"

If _____, then _____.

The format of this content principle will help you recognize it when you see one. A principle can usually be phrased in an "If_____ then _____" statement. Following the "if" is the cause. Following the "then" is the effect. "If you face your teacher squarely and lean toward her, then you are paying attention." Cause and effect. "If you outline your paper before writing it, your ideas will build upon each other." **The "if" is the skill step you are teaching your learners, while the "then" is the skill itself.** Your learners can now understand how the skill steps work.

A second kind of principle describes why something is important to the learner. It hooks up the content with the learners' frames of reference. The principle does this by answering the question "How will the learner benefit from this skill?" "If you face your teacher squarely and lean toward her, then you are paying attention so that you will hear and see all that she is saying." "If you outline your paper before writing it, then your ideas will build upon each other so that you won't be at a loss for what to write next." If (*skill steps*), then (*skill*) so that (*learner benefit*). This second kind of principle extends the idea of cause and effect. Doing the skill becomes the "cause" and the learner benefit becomes the "effect."

Your learners need to learn principles so that they can apply what they learn.

It will be sufficient for you to write one principle for each daily skill content. That principle should link the skill steps to the learner. You will write the principle of what steps lead to the skill being performed which, in turn, leads to the learner benefit. For example, "If you tell when and where a short story took place, then you will describe the setting of the story so that you prepare the reader to understand what happened in it." Examining this last principle, you will note that the "cause" is really the skill step. The "effect" is performing the skill. This, in turn, leads to the learner benefit. Very simply, then, you can write a principle for your daily content using the format: If (*skill steps*) then (*skill*) so that (*learner benefit*).

COURSE

I.   Unit

   A. Topic

      1. Task

         a.   Skill (*Principle*)

            1) Step

               a) Facts

               b) Concepts

            2) Step

               a) Facts

               b) Concepts

            3) Step

               a) Facts

               b) Concepts

I.   Learning Skills
    A.   Exploring the Learning
        1.   Attending to the learning
            a.   Attending physically (If you square, lean forward and stop distractions, then you will attend physically so that you will know that you are ready to see and hear the teacher and the learning materials.)

    1)   Posture squarely in relation to teacher or learning materials.
        a)   Facts: teacher, learning materials
        b)   Concepts: posture, squarely

    2)   Lean forward.
        a)   Facts: none
        b)   Concepts: lean, forward

    3)   Stop distracting motions.
        a)   Facts: distracting motions
        b)   Concepts: none

    4)   Make eye contact with teacher or materials.
        a)   Facts: eye contact
        b)   Concepts: none

Using a Model to Develop a Principle

Don scratched his head thoughtfully as he examined his daily content. "If my kids do the steps of this skill, what effect will it have on them?" he asked himself aloud. "I guess they would know that they'd be ready to see and hear the teacher and the learning materials." Then Don used the format to write: "If you square, lean forward and stop distractions, then you will attend physically, so that you will know that you are ready to see and hear the teacher and the learning materials.

Sandra had little trouble inserting such a principle into her program.

I.   Using Counting Numbers
    A.   Understanding Place Value
        1.   Ordering the numbers
            a.   Stating greater than relationships ' > ' (If you put the larger number first and the smaller second, then you will be stating a greater than relationship so that you will understand how to put numbers in order by size.)

    1)   Draw number line to include the two numbers being compared.
        a)   Facts: number line, number
        b)   Concepts: compared

    2)   Find number farthest to right.
        a)   Facts: none
        b)   Concepts: farthest, right

    3)   Write that greater number, then symbol, and finally the smaller number — to left on number line.
        a)   Facts: symbol
        b)   Concepts: left, greater, smaller

    4)   Read what you have written to self.
        a)   Facts: none
        b)   Concepts: read

Using the format "If (*skill step*), then (*skill*) so that (*learner benefit*)," write a principle for your daily skill. This statement will tend to link the skill and skill steps to the learner.

COURSE:_____

UNIT:_____

TOPIC:_____

TASK:_____

SKILL:_____

PRINCIPLE:_____

STEP 1:_____

FACTS:_____

CONCEPTS:_____

STEP 2:_____

FACTS:_____

CONCEPTS:_____

STEP 3: _____

    FACTS: _____

    CONCEPTS: _____

STEP 4: _____

    FACTS: _____

    CONCEPTS: _____

"Well," sighed Sandra, "I've written the content for one skill, but I'm just not too confident about doing the assignment."

"I could use a review myself, Sandy," Don added. "Tell me about facts!"

Sandra went to the board and spoke as she wrote: "Names of people, places and things. In other words, facts are nouns, right?"

Don nodded his head. "Concepts are all the other words — the verbs, adverbs, prepositions and adjectives. Concepts are ideas we have about facts."

"Oh, I like that, Don. Facts are labels, and concepts are ideas about those labels." Sandra turned once more to the board and wrote "principle." She tossed the chalk into the air. "I've got it. The principle states two relationships. Internally, it relates the skill steps to the skill. And externally it relates the skill to the learner."

"Hey, wait a minute," interrupted Don. "Run that by me again."

"Remember, cause and effect? The principle states an effect in terms of skills and benefits. Steps cause skills, and skills cause benefits. See what I mean, Don?" questioned Sandra.

"Yeah, but the format we learned is really the best way to remember how to write principles." Don shuffled through his notes. "Here it is." And he wrote: "If (*skill step*) then (*skill*) so that (*learner benefit*)."

"Okay," said Don. "That takes care of the supportive knowledge. But at some point we're going to be tested on everything — the steps and skills as well as the yearly content."

"That's going to be a tough test, Don. Let's review it together so that we'll have all the pieces." Sandra turned to the board and wrote the following:

COURSE

```
                        ⎧  I.  Unit
Five Levels             ⎪      A.  Topic
     of                 ⎨          1.  Task
Yearly Content          ⎪              a.  Skill
                        ⎩                  Principle      ⎫
                                       1)  Step           ⎪
                                           a)  Fact       ⎬   Five Levels
                                           b)  Concept    ⎪        of
                                                          ⎭   Daily Content
```

"This is how I remember what my content should look like," said Sandra. "I know that there are five levels to my yearly content, and five levels to the daily one."

"And where the first level ends with a 'skill,' the daily content begins with a 'skill,'" added Don.

Sandra began to gather up her books and papers, then suddenly stopped. "Well, for heaven's sake, of all the sneaky . . ." She grinned at Don who looked at her as if she had three heads. "I've got it, Don, 'The Scale'! — how to rate those darn pre- and post-tests."

"You mean it, Sandy?" Don asked.

"Sure, you need five levels — right?"

1.0 — Very Ineffective

2.0 — Ineffective

3.0 — Minimally Effective

4.0 — Very Effective

5.0 — Extremely Effective

"Now watch this," said Sandra, excited, as she added:

1.0 — Very Ineffective — Facts

2.0 — Ineffective — Facts and Concepts

3.0 — Minimally Effective — Facts, Concepts and Principles

4.0 — Very Effective — Facts, Concepts, Principles and Skills

5.0 — Extremely Effective — Facts, Concepts, Principles, Skills and Skill Steps

"Well, I'll be . . . You've got it, Sandy. Just wait till we get that post-test. We'll cream it!"

Sandra and Don spent many hours writing out the supportive knowledge for their first units. By the time they were done, they were confident of their abilities to develop personalized content for their learners. They had reinforced what they had learned with practice; and in doing so, they had acquired a new set of teaching skills.

To ensure that you master these content development skills, practice on the unit you wrote in the previous chapter. Write the supportive knowledge for each skill in that unit.

179 POST-TRAINING CONTENT DEVELOPMENT ASSESS-MENT

Now that you understand the five-point rating scale, you will probably not be intimidated by the communication task. Write out the daily content for a skill of your choice. Develop the steps and the supportive knowledge for that skill. In other words, include the facts, concepts, principles, skill and skill steps of your daily content.

SKILL: _____

Writing your daily skills content may have been easy for you. The amount of practice you have had increased your confidence in your new-found skill. See if you can use these new skills to evaluate existing content. As a classroom teacher, you will find most of your content already developed in one form or another. You need to be able to discriminate if these contents are effective. To do this, check out your discriminations of the following five contents by using the five-point scale.

1.0 — Very Ineffective

2.0 — Ineffective

3.0 — Minimally Effective

4.0 — Very Effective

5.0 — Extremely Effective

You may use a rating more than once. If you judge a content as falling between two ratings, you may split the difference and use 1.5, 2.5, 3.5 or 4.5.

Your Rating:_____

Skill: Reading lines of latitude

(If you can find the equator and count the number of lines in the direction of the correct pole, then you can read lines of latitude so that you will know how far south or north of the equator you are.)

1. Find the equator.

2. If N, then go toward North Pole.

3. If S, then go toward South Pole.

4. Find correct latitude and point it out with left hand.

Your Rating:_____

Skill: Brushing Your Teeth

(If you can apply the paste and brush all surfaces thoroughly, then you can brush your teeth so that you will reduce the chances of cavities).

1. Moisten toothbrush.
   a) Toothbrush —
   b) Moisten — hold under water

2. Apply toothpaste.
   a) Toothpaste —
   b) Apply — squeeze 1/2 inch of paste onto bristles

3. Brush upper, outside surfaces.
   a) Brush — up and down motion
   b) Upper, outside — the part of the teeth you see when you smile

4. Brush upper, inside surfaces.
   a) Inside — the part you don't see when you smile.

5. Brush upper chewing surfaces.
   a) Chewing surfaces — the part that touches the bottom teeth

6. Spit.

7. Repeat #3-6 for lower teeth.
   a) Lower — bottom

8. Rinse with glass of water.
   a) Rinse — swish in clear water

CONTENT C

Your Rating: _____

Skill: Finding Important Words When Reading

1.   Skim chapter to find words in dark print or italics.
     a.   Italics — Slanted print which looks different from the words around it
     b.   Skim — glance through quickly, starting from the top down

2.   Read to define the word in dark print or italics.
     a.   Define — tell what the word means

3.   Read subheadings under pictures or charts.
     a.   Subheadings — the caption or sentences directly under the picture or chart

4.   Determine the idea in illustrations.
     a.   Illustrations — map, picture or chart
     b.   Idea — why something's important or what it says

5.   Describe the illustrations.

Your Rating: _____

Skill: Sketching a Map

(If you can make a line drawing that approximates the shape of your country, then you can sketch a map.)

1. Place a model U. S. map on a flip chart in front of the class.

2. Indicate major features of the East Coast, such as Cape Cod and Florida.
    a. East Coast — right-hand side of map bordering on Atlantic Ocean
    b. Cape Cod and Florida — peninsula
    c. Indicate — point out on model

3. Indicate major features of Southern border, such as Gulf of Mexico and Texas.
    a. Gulf of Mexico
    b. Texas
    c. Southern — bottom of U. S.

4. Indicate length of West Coast in relation to East Coast.
    a. West Coast — left-hand side of map bordering on Pacific Ocean

5. Indicate major features of Northern border, such as Great Lakes and Maine.
    a. Northern — top of U. S. bordering Canada
    b. Great Lakes — five lakes 1/4 of the way from East Coast

Your Rating:_____

Skill: Understanding the Problems of Pioneers

(If you understand the circumstances involved in
pioneering, then you will appreciate the hardships of
the American Pioneer.)

1. Map the early pioneer routes — Northern and Southern — from Independence, Missouri.
    a.   Oregon Trail — Platte River, Wyoming, Idaho to Oregon
    b.   Sante Fe Trail — New Mexico, Arizona to California

2. Discuss the geographical considerations of each route.
    a.   Plains — rolling grasslands with little cover
    b.   Mountains — weather and passes
    c.   Desert — no water and a compass

3. Give students a map and compass to follow a trail through woods.
    a.   Compass — indicate the magnetic North Pole
    b.   Follow — match map cues with those on trail

You probably felt much more confident while rating these contents. Now you would like to compare your ratings to those of the trained raters. Again, to obtain your post-test discrimination score, write the difference between your score and the trained raters' ratings. Then add these differences and divide the sum by 5.

Content	Ratings	Your Ratings		Differences
A	1.0	- _____	=	_____
B	5.0	- _____	=	_____
C	2.0	- _____	=	_____
D	4.0	- _____	=	_____
E	3.0	- _____	=	_____
		Total = _____	=	_____
			5	Content Development Discrimination Score

If your discrimination score is more than .5, you should re-read Chapter Four before going further in the text. Select another unit to practice the skills, giving yourself additional exercise. This may seem to be too much work, but it is a waste of your time unless you do everything you can to master these new skills.

You might have grown accustomed by now, to using the explanation of the ratings to review what you have learned. These explanations help you to see how well you have learned these content development skills. As you have already noted, Content B, Brushing Your Teeth, received a 'very effective' rating of 5.0 because it contained the five levels of daily content development: facts, concepts, principles, skill and skill steps. The 4.0 content of sketching a map was effective to the extent that it contained the facts, concepts and principles the learners would need to do the skill; however, the content did not break it down into the steps the learners required if they were to do the skill. Content E, presenting the problems of pioneers, rated 3.0 or 'minimally effective.' That is because its content was made up of supportive knowledge only. "Understanding Problems" is not a skill nor can it be broken into steps instructing the learners how to perform "understanding." Content C rated a 2.0, because it did not include a principle for finding the important words while reading. If the content does not include all of these elements, its rating will be lower than 5.0. This is why Content A received a rating of 1.0, or 'extremely ineffective.' For without the necessary supportive facts and concepts, the learners would not be able to learn the new skills.

Understanding Daily Content

Now you should know that there are five levels to develop in a day's content. After selecting the **skill** of the day, you break that skill into **skill steps**. The skill is what you want the learners to be able to do. The skill steps are the steps the learners will take to perform the skill. There are reasons that a skill works the way it does, and these reasons are the **principles** which make up part of the daily content. The last two levels of the daily content are found within the skill steps. These are the **facts** and **concepts** which the learner must learn to perform the steps successfully.

The five levels of daily content detail the yearly content. This detail assures your learners of a year's intellectual growth.

Level 1 — Facts

Level 2 — Facts and Concepts

Level 3 — Facts, Concepts and Principles

Level 4 — Facts, Concepts, Principles and Skill

Level 5 — Facts, Concepts, Principles, Skill and
           Skill Steps

With mastery of daily content development, will come an increase in teaching effectiveness. No longer will you teach facts one day and concepts another, with an occasional principle thrown in with a skill. Your content now has a focus: the **skill**. That focuses the content on what you want the learners to be able to do. The content will be more effective because there is a reason for teaching the facts, concepts and principles the students need to perform the skill. Skill **steps** increase your effectiveness, because they state in detail what the learners should do in order to perform the skill. The picture that you sketched in outlining yearly content, has been completed, in detail, with the daily content. It remains to be seen how you will deliver that picture to the learners. But you can already feel confident that your content is ready.

Before Class: "You said we'd learn how to write a simple sentence today. That sounds like it might not be so simple!"

"You're a little afraid because you're not sure you're going to be able to do it."

After Class: "Hey, that wasn't so hard at all!"

"Now you feel good about yourself because you got it right!"

Your content development skills provide daily growth for your learners

"Hi, Mandy."

"Huh? Oh, hi, Larissa. What's happening?"

"Well, you remember that old light box we made last year for our science project?"

"Oh, yeah, sure! Where is that thing, anyway?"

"I've got it at home. But listen — I took it in to my new teacher, Mr. Thompson, and he explained the whole thing to me step by step! It's really neat!"

"Yeah? What'd he say?"

"Well, he showed me how those Christmas lights work. Each one's got a little thing called a 'heat resistor' in it. So when each light heats up enough, it turns off and waits until it's cool enough to go back on again. And because each resistor's a little different, all the lights blink on and off at their own rate!"

"So? What's that mean?"

"Dummy! It means that the pattern the lights make on the screen is a random one. You remember how we always felt like the lights were blinking in time with whatever music we put on? Well, that was because our ears would hear a beat in the music and our eyes would automatically pick up the random blinking light that was going on right then. Mr. Thompson said our box demonstrated the coordination of visual and auditory stimuli!"

"Yeah? Huh! Maybe I can switch into his class after Christmas — he sounds pretty smart!"

Effective content supports your learners' acquisition of new skills by including facts, concepts, and principles!

SECTION III. UNDERSTANDING TEACHING PREPARATION

5

191

CHAPTER 5: TEACHING YOUR CONTENT

Content Development Skills Ensure Effectiveness

In your first teaching assignment, the preparation may consume much of your time. You will be unfamiliar with the new content and the twenty-five or so children in your class. It is very important to you that you not make mistakes. Organizing your yearly content assures you that your teaching will be coherent and directionful from one week to the next.

You may spend several hours every night planning the content and the methods to be used the next day. Teaching this daily content provides your learners with the source of a year's growth! You help them to acquire 120 — or more — new skills by teaching the skill steps and the supportive knowledge they need to learn effectively.

If you develop your content effectively, then your teaching will touch your learners.

In the first chapter, you attempted to develop the content of a daily lesson. Your efforts were probably less than perfect and with good reason — you had not yet learned content development skills. Now that you have these skills, you will want to measure your growth by selecting another small piece of content to outline in 20 or 30 minutes. You will want to develop this content as you would prepare it for a class you would teach. Again include the following content development objectives in your content:

First, show how this content fits into the yearly content. Include the course title, unit, and the part of the unit that this lesson is taken from.

Second, describe what skill your learners would have learned previous to this lesson.

Third, list the skill that you will teach.

Fourth, write out all the steps needed to perform the new skill.

Fifth, define any terms or facts the learners may need to understand in order to perform the steps.

CONTENT OUTLINE FOR ONE LESSON:

Just as you measured your discriminations of developed content in the first chapter, you should, at this point, measure your discriminations again. You will want to compare these two scores to tell yourself what you have learned. It will be important to make good judgments about content in selecting textbooks and other learning materials. Measure your judgments or discriminations by rating the five different contents which follow on a scale of 1 to 5 as below:

1.0 — Very Ineffective

2.0 — Ineffective

3.0 — Minimally Effective

4.0 — Very Effective

5.0 — Extremely Effective

If you feel a response falls between two levels on a five-point scale, rate it as 1.5, 2.5, 3.5 or 4.5. You may use a rating more than once.

Your Rating:_____

Course Title: Handwriting

  Unit: Manuscript Letters

    Topic: Horizontal and Vertical Lines

      Task: Capital Letters

        Skill: Printing "I," "L" and "T"

(If your vertical lines are truly vertical, your letters will stand at attention.)

(If your horizontal lines are truly horizontal, they will look strong and solid.)

1) Print "I," following model.
   a) One vertical line (straight up and down)
   b) Two horizontal lines (straight left to right)

2) Print "L," following model.
   a) One vertical line
   b) One horizontal line

3) Print "T," following model.
   a) One vertical line
   b) One horizontal line

Your Rating:_____

Course Title: General Science

   Unit: The Human Body

      Topic: Digestion

         Task: The Food Passage

            Skill: Learning the Major Organs in the Alimentary Canal to Describe Digestion

(If you can learn the organs and know their functions, then you will be able to trace food from the moment it is eaten until it enters the blood stream, so that you understand what happens to the food you eat.)

1) Mouth — prepares the food for the stomach by chewing and some enzyme action on starches.
   a) Teeth
   b) Tongue
   c) Salivary Glands

2) Esophagus — carries food to stomach.

3) Stomach — food further digested by gastric juices, also churned by peristalsis.

4) Pylorus — valve at end of stomach before small intestines.

5) Small Intestine (22 - 25 ft. long) — more digestion by juices.
   a) Villi — absorb food into blood and lymph

6) Large Intestine — absorbs water into body and excretes waste.

Your Rating: _____

Course Title: Social Studies

    Unit: Geography of South America

       Topic: Natural Resources

          Task: Map Reading

            Skill: Brazil

1) Hilly Uplands
   a) Farming
   b) Salt

2) Plateaus
   a) Lumbering
   b) Grasslands

3) Low Mountains
   a) Iron Ore
   b) Quartz Crystals
   c) Industrial Diamonds
   d) Lead
   e) Tin
   f) Tungsten
   g) Chrome Ores
   h) Mica
   i) Gold

198   CONTENT D

Your Rating:_____

Course Title: Mathematics

  Unit: Decimal Fractions

    Topic: Addition of Decimal Fractions

      Task: Understanding Place Value

        Skill: Reading Decimals to the Thousandths Place

        (If you can name the place values of decimal fractions, then you can always have a common denominator by adding zero place holders.)

        1) The third place to the right of the decimal point is named the thousandths place.
           a) Decimal Point — separates whole numbers from fractional numbers
           b) Right — ⟶
           c) Thousandths — 1/1000

        2) Read the numeral and name the place.
           a) Numeral — combination of digits that name a number
           b) Place — 3 spaces to the right of the decimal point is the thousandths place.

        3) Write a fraction that expresses the name of the decimal fraction and ask yourself if that is the name of the decimal fraction.

Your Rating:_____

Course Title: Reading: Level #3

    Unit: Phonics

        Topic: Vowel Sounds

            Task: Short Vowels

                Skill: 'a'

1) Copy following list
   a) Apple
   b) Ate
   c) Am
   d) Aim
   e) Act

2) Identify those words that begin with short 'a'.

3) Write three words that have a short 'a' middle sound

4) Spell the following words using short 'a'.
   a) Pat
   b) Fat
   c) Ham
   d) Mast
   e) Fast
   f) Task

You may be eager to get some idea of how well you did in rating the content. The feedback on your ability to discriminate effective from ineffective content follows.

Trained raters who have demonstrated the validity of their ratings in studies of teaching outcome rated each of the contents in terms of its level of development. These ratings are listed in the table below. You may now wish to determine your discrimination score.

Your Score:

Content	Ratings	Your Ratings	Difference (*Deviation from Ratings*)
A	4.0	- _____ =	_____
B	3.0	- _____ =	_____
C	1.0	- _____ =	_____
D	5.0	- _____ =	_____
E	2.0	- _____ =	_____
		Total =	_____

$$\frac{}{5} = \underline{\hspace{3cm}}$$

Content
Development
Discrimination
Score

One-half level of deviation from the trained raters rating is considered a good discrimination score. This means that while the trained rater rates an item at level 3.0, you might rate it as 2.5 or 3.5. If your discrimination score is off more than one-half level from that of the raters', you should go back and learn these skills again.

Understanding the Discrimination Scores

Once again you will want to examine our explanation of the discrimination score. You understand that there are five levels of daily content. A level 1.0 content is indicated by its exclusive use of facts. An example of this is Content C, Social Studies, which is simply a list of Brazil's natural resources. To move to a level of 2.0, the content must contain not only facts, but concepts as well. Content E, Reading, is an example of a 2.0 content, for it contains the facts and concepts concerning short 'a,' but loses effectiveness by including several skills, and no skill steps or principle. A level 3.0 content is one which contains the facts, concepts, and a principle. Content B, General Science, received this rating. It contains the facts and concepts of the digestive system, as well as a principle for understanding these facts and concepts. However, 'knowing' is not a skill, and therefore the content contains no skill steps. The fourth level of content is illustrated by Content A, Handwriting. Its only deficit is that the following of a model may or may not be a skill step. If the model indicated that the vertical line of an 'I' should be drawn before the horizontal lines, then the content would be 'extremely effective.' However, these skill steps are absent from this content. The most effective content is Content D, Mathematics, which contains five levels of content. Receiving a rating of 5.0, this content includes the facts, concepts, principles and skill steps of the skill: "reading a decimal to the thousandths place."

Understanding the Communication Scores

With this explanation, you can go back to your communication post-test and rate your ability to develop content. Your content should be inclusive. In other words, a content must include **facts** as well as **concepts**, to rate 2.0. A skills content containing only skill steps rates a 1.0 because it does not contain the supportive knowledge the learners need to perform the skill. Compare your pre-test (from Chapter One) and post-test communication score by recording them below.

Pre-Test Communication Score: _____

Post-Test Communication Score: _____

There are so many things to do when you teach. Developing the content is the first step — there are so many other skills you will need! And yet, without a content you have nothing to teach. Your teaching methods and classroom management could not exist independently of the content. When you organize your yearly content, you paint a large picture of that content. It is a sketch with initial lines and broad shapes that make up that content. Then you detail your picture with the daily content. In this way, you and your learners can distinguish the specifics of the picture that you paint each day when you teach.

PHASES OF TEACHING

		I	II	III
TEACHING PREPARATION:	Developing Content			

Diagnosis

Once you have broken the yearly content into daily skills, steps, principles, concepts and facts, you can prepare for teaching. Your first step will be to diagnose your learners in respect to this content. Perhaps your learners have already acquired certain skills included in the content. In that case, it would be redundant to teach those skills again. Other learners may not have sufficient skills to perform even the first daily skill of your content. You may have to develop another, more appropriate content for them. Still other learners may be just ready to begin learning the very first skill of your yearly content. The diagnosis will give you this information.

Teachers diagnose their learners informally every day. They draw conclusions about their learners.

"Marguerite reads very well but cannot remember her number facts."

"Tony has trouble organizing his notes."

"Sarah has to work very hard!"

Teachers diagnose their learners more formally when they test them. A pre-test or a post-test will indicate if the learners have the necessary abilities to learn the new skills. These diagnoses give teachers the information they require when planning their classes.

PHASES OF TEACHING

		I	II	III
TEACHING PREPARATION:	Developing Content	▶ Diagnosing		

If you diagnose your learners effectively, then you will understand them.

Accumulating the results of your diagnosis, you will draw certain conclusions. You may decide that the learners are all ready to begin at the same place in the content. Perhaps you will divide them into small groups, to begin at various places in the content. For individualized instruction, each learner may be placed at a different point in relation to the content. In any case, you have set an initial goal for the learners. You have, in effect, said "You will learn **this** skill first."

PHASES OF TEACHING

		I	II	III
TEACHING PREPARATION:	Developing Content ▶	Diagnosing ▶	Goal-Setting	

If you set appropriate goals for your learners, then you can meet their individual needs.

Having decided where each learner should begin in the content, you will sit down and plan your lessons. You will decide what methods to use to overview the new skill. Your learners should be able to listen to instructions and see how the skill steps are performed. Planning a video tape and arranging a live demonstration, are just two of the many methods that you may select to do this. Searching through past experience, you will decide how your learners should practice the new skill. You may ditto a worksheet, plan a laboratory or have the learners engage in a hands-on experience. Not only will you want to use a variety of methods, but you will also want to use a variety of sensory inputs. Your methods will reflect auditory, visual, and kinesthetic techniques as you plan the delivery of your lessons.

PHASES OF TEACHING

	I	II	III
TEACHING PREPARATION:	Developing Content ▶ Diagnosing ▶	Goal Setting ▶	Lesson Planning

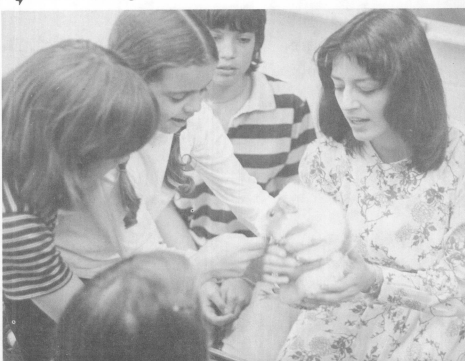

If you plan effective lessons, then the learners will want to learn.

Attending

Armed with your content and methods, you are ready to make a teaching delivery to the learners. You know what skills they need to learn and you have prepared the methods you will use to teach these skills. As you begin, you will attend to your learners. By attending, we mean making **observations** about their readiness to learn and noting the way they feel. Checking to see if they are attending to you and if their materials are ready for use are ways that you determine their readiness: John's got his head down — he's not ready; but Marcie is sitting up straight and looking right at you — she's ready for anything! You will **listen** to the learners when you attend. They may indicate by noise level, individual comments or questions whether they are ready to begin or are still out on the baseball field.

When you attend, you will decide if your learners are up or down, ready or not ready to begin.

PHASES OF TEACHING

		I	II	III
TEACHING PREPARATION:	Developing Content	▶ Diagnosing	▶ Goal Setting	▶ Lesson Planning
TEACHING DELIVERY:	Attending			

If you attend to your learners, then they will know you are ready to begin.

Responding

Having determined that your learners are ready to learn, you will begin teaching. That delivery will be characterized by a two-way communication between you and the learners. You will **respond** to their verbal questions and answers. Noting various learner behaviors, you will respond to whether the learners are still with you; and most importantly, you will respond to the learners' performances of the new skill. It is at the responding level that **you** explore what the learners understand and what they do not.

"So Jimmy, you're saying that you understand what we'll do next. And Helen, you feel pretty good about your ability to do it right."

PHASES OF TEACHING

		I	II	III
TEACHING PREPARATION:	Developing Content	▶ Diagnosing	▶ Goal Setting	▶ Lesson Planning
		▽		
TEACHING DELIVERY:	Attending	▶ Responding		
		▽		
		Exploring		

If you respond to your learners, then you can explore what they know with them.

After you respond to the learners, you will assess what they understand and what they do not. You will **personalize** your learners' responses. Drawing conclusions from what you see and hear, you may decide that the learners are ready for the next step or method or a new step or new method.

"They still don't understand how the pieces fit together. They need more practice."

"They really can do that well. Now they are ready to apply the new skill."

"They've got everything but the last step. I'll have to break that step down into two steps."

When you personalize, you try to match your learners to the part of the content and methods appropriate to them. You understand what your learners need.

PHASES OF TEACHING

		I	II	III
TEACHING PREPARATION:	Developing Content	▶ Diagnosing	▶ Goal Setting	▶ Lesson Planning
TEACHING DELIVERY:	Attending	▶ Responding	▶ Personalizing	
		Exploring	Understanding	

If you personalize your delivery, then you will reach all of the learners.

Personalizing Requires You to Recognize Feelings

Each of your learners experiences many different feelings every day: happy feelings and sad ones, angry feelings or feelings of confusion and just plain fear. Before you can really personalize things for your learners, you've got to use your attending skills of observing and listening to identify these feelings.

Is Kevin slumped in his seat, eyes down, not looking at you or anyone else, not even looking at his text? Chances are he's really down about something, really depressed. Could it be he's having trouble with the material?

Lucia has her hand up every time you ask a question. She's smiling and practically bouncing in her seat with eagerness to share some new understanding with you and the class. She must be very pleased, even excited, to be acting in this way. What specific word or phrase seems to "capture" her feeling in a way that she could understand?

Personalizing also Means Recognizing How Learner Feelings are Related To Content

Not all of your learners' feelings will be related to your content, or even to school in general, of course. But quite often learners' appearances and behaviors reflect feelings that **are** the direct result of their interacting with content — with the skills, the skill steps, the facts, concepts and principles which you are presenting. You must be able to recognize the link between feelings and content before you can frame a personalized response.

Cindy was all smiles until you handed back the latest worksheets. She got a pretty low grade. Now she has stopped smiling and won't even look at her neighbor. Her worksheet gets stuffed into her desk. Her eyes look teary. Surely her feeling of sadness is related to her poor performance. Indeed, these two factors form two sides of a simple equation: "Cindy feels sad because she performed poorly."

Benito has worked diligently for ten minutes on the new worksheet. You've watched him writing away, lost in his work. Then he finishes and comes running up to your desk with his paper, grinning broadly, the first to finish. Here you can piece together another equation, this time a positive one: "Benito feels proud because he finished his work first."

Because you have developed our content in terms of specific skills and skill steps, you will be able to respond to our learners in ways that personalize their individual problems — and individual triumphs — in these areas. Here's where your interpersonal skills of observing and listening really pay off! Noting the way a particular learner seems to feel, you can select an appropriate "feeling" word or phrase (*usually one which reflects one intensity or another of happiness, sorrow, anger, confusion or fear*) and use this term to link the learner up with the content with which she or he is dealing.

"You're really happy because you found out you can handle these long-division problems" (*personalizing the learner's acquisition of a new skill*); or, "You're pretty angry because you can't seem to do long-division every time" (*personalizing the learner's problem with a new skill*).

"You're proud of yourself for identifying all the verbs correctly" (*personalizing the learner's successful completion of a skill step*); or, "You're feeling lost because you can't tell which of the words in the sentences are verbs" (*personalizing the learner's problem with a particular skill step*).

Personalizing the Learner's Experience with Facts, Concepts and Principles

Learners react emotionally to facts, concepts and principles just as they do to their efforts with larger skill steps and overall skills. Here again, your personalized response can help link specific feelings to specific content.

"Linda, you're mad at yourself because you thought you knew the capital of New York State and now you can't remember" (*personalizing a learner's feeling concerning a specific fact*).

"Jimmy, it seems like you're confused because you didn't realize we were only supposed to be finding out about meat-eating or carnivorous animals" (*personalizing a learner's feeling about a concept*).

"Annette, you must feel just great because you finally see that shifting a decimal point to the right one place is the same as multiplying the original number by 10" (*personalizing a learner's feeling related to a principle*).

Now you can do more than simply develop effective content. You can help your learners deal more effectively with that content by personalizing their problems and triumphs. In this way, you show the learners where they are — and you also show them that you're right there with them in terms of your individual understanding and awareness. You're not just teaching — you're helping them learn!

First you attend in order to identify the individual learner's unique feeling, taking your cue from specific behaviors and/or appearances. Sara's scowling and glaring at her just-returned assignment; she looks **mad**.

Next you identify what if any aspect of your content has given rise to the feeling. Sara usually masters new skills quite easily; today, however, she has had trouble writing topic sentences for paragraphs.

Finally, you respond in a way that shows the learner you understand — and a way that puts her or him in control of things! "Sara, I guess you're pretty mad because you had a hard time getting your topic sentences right."

You're not ignoring the learner. Nor are you giving empty advice or talking like an all-wise adult. Instead, you are really saying something like "I know how you feel — see? And I know you feel that way because of something you did or didn't do — see?"

In personalizing your responses to learners, your aim is to do much more than just to reflect an awareness of learner problems. You personalize with learners so that **they** can see what's really going on, what's really contributing to their feelings — and so you, in the end, can honestly personalize the most positive and heart-felt response possible: "You feel really great because you've learned so much!"

You're not above or beyond your learners. You're not teaching **at** them. Instead, you're right there with them, caring all the time; and your personalized response makes this very clear indeed!

Cumulatively, then, you will attend, respond and personalize so that you can **initiate**. And what do you initiate . . . more teaching preparation. You will develop additional content, diagnose, set goals and plan more effective methods to deliver that content. Initiating is what will make the difference for your learners. You act to make your teaching relevant for your learners.

PHASES OF TEACHING

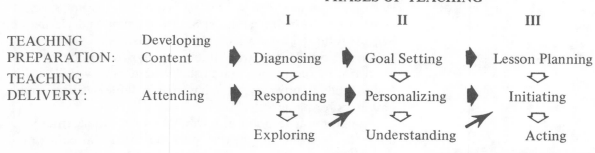

		I	II	III
TEACHING PREPARATION:	Developing Content	Diagnosing	Goal Setting	Lesson Planning
TEACHING DELIVERY:	Attending	Responding	Personalizing	Initiating
		Exploring	Understanding	Acting

If you act with your teaching delivery skills, then you will be a creative teacher.

So we come full circle with our phases of teaching. Starting with a developed and personalized content, you will prepare to teach that content. Your preparation involves exploring, understanding and acting on what and how to teach that content to your learners. That is your preparation. Then you are ready to deliver that content with methods that you have selected. Again, you explore, understand and act with respect to the learners' reactions to the content and methods. When you act, you cycle back to teaching preparation, beginning with content development.

PHASES OF TEACHING

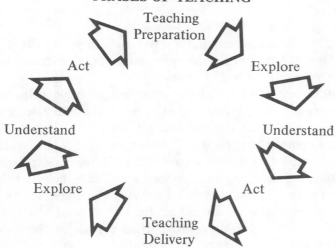

September.

Marty took the seat next to Tim, whose expression was one of suppressed glee. "We made it!"

"Told you, didn't I?" Tim was equally gleeful. The two friends had just come back from lunch with the rest of the class on this, their first day in 5th grade. "Hey, Miz James seems O.K., huh?"

"Yeah, maybe . . ." Marty didn't want to commit himself yet. "It's kinda soon to tell."

"Oh, sure! But she was sayin' the first thing she wants to do is just find out what we already know. That's cool! Heck, the first day last year old Miz Principato just let us talk about how we spent the summer and dumb stuff like that!"

"Yeah, and Mr. Huston just charged right in with all kinds of work without ever knowing whether we were smart or stupid or what," Marty agreed. He thought back to the way their new teacher, Miz James, had been that morning — like she was really right there with them, not pushing but not holding anything back either.

"Did you understand that stuff about roads and maps she was saying?" Tim asked.

"Sure — she meant that getting through a school year is like taking a trip somewhere in a car. Before you can figure out where you want to go, you gotta know where you are right now!"

Tim nodded. The teacher's comments had made sense to him, too. Marty was right, it was too soon to really tell about Miz James yet. But Tim was starting to get a good feeling about their new teacher already. Maybe this year would be O.K.. At least it couldn't be much dumber than last year!

January.

It had started to snow again, the large white flakes sweeping down out of the iron-gray sky and silently joining the six or so inches that had fallen the day before. Few of the 5th graders had noticed the new snow, however. Most of them were clustered around three long tables near the back of the room, talking together in hushed undertones as they worked to get the small model engines running.

Then the voices around one of the tables rose in angry disagreement. Almost at once two figures broke away from the table and headed for Miz James.

"Miz Janes, tell Marty he's crazy, will you?" Tim's voice cracked with frustration. So did Marty's as he added his two-bits.

"You're dumb! Miz James, Tim's got our engine all fouled up!"

Ms. James crouched before the two boys and looked them over. "Well, you guys are pretty upset about something, huh? What seems to be the problem?"

Talking over and under and around each other, Tim and Marty explained the foul-up. It seemed that they were at odds about how to fill the small radiator on their model internal combustion engine. Tim argued for plain water. Marty wanted to mix the water with anti-freeze. Miz James responded to their separate concerns and then helped them sort things out. They wouldn't be trying the engines outside until tomorrow she explained. So for today, plain water was fine. Then tomorrow they could drain a little of the water and add some anti-freeze, an essential precaution if the engines were going to be protected against the winter's sub-freezing temperatures.

"I guess we should have figured that out, huh?" Marty speculated a while later.

"Yeah, I guess so." Tim was tightening the miniature fan belt. "Man, I never thought we could learn this much about engines and motors and stuff!"

"Me neither! You should have seen my Dad's face when I started talking to him last night about how carburetors mix air and gas and stuff like that — he was really knocked out!"

"Yeah, mine too — especially when I told him that the best person in the whole class at setting up a motor was Cissy Ferguson. He couldn't believe that a 5th grade girl could be that smart!"

"Your father's not being fair," Marty said. "Mine isn't either. Cissy's really smart!"

Tim nodded. "Yeah, but we're all gettin' smarter this year. I never learned so much in my life!" He meant it, too.

June.

"Hey, Miz James, this is the last unit we're gonna work on, huh?"

Ms. James nodded. "That's right, Marty. I know it's sort of sad because the year's almost over, and there are still so many things we could do. But there'll be more chances next year when you're in 6th grade."

Marty nodded. Sitting next to him, Tim was thinking back over all the different units of work they had done that year. Units in Math, English, Social Studies and Science. Projects like working with the model engines. Like figuring out how much money it would take to live in a certain way. Like writing letters to people at the Town Hall and getting back answers! All kinds of stuff. Almost all of it had been fun, Tim thought. Oh, sure, there had been days when he hadn't felt like coming to school. Who wants to be in school on the first really nice spring day after a long miserable winter? But there had been a lot fewer days like that this year than last — a whole lot fewer! Tim felt good about this year. He felt like he was a lot more grown up, like he understood a lot of things better than he had before. He was glad summer was here, but for the first time in who knows how long, he found himself thinking that it might not be so bad to start school again in September. Not really bad. In a way, it might even be good . . .

Beside him, Marty put into words a question that Tim had been about to ask.

"Hey Miz James?"

"Marty?"

"Miz James, what grade are you gonna teach next year . . .?"

July.

Once again, Gail Swenson sat at her desk and surveyed the year-end batch of achievement tests. This time she was reviewing the 5th grade's performance.

Once again the weather outside was hot and humid. But this year the school's antiquated air conditioning system seemed to be holding its own.

"And so is the 5th grade," Gail murmured to herself with very real pleasure. "In fact, I really don't know how things could have gone much better for them . . ."

BIBLIOGRAPHY

Aspy, D.N.
Toward a Technology for Humanizing Education
Champaign, Illinois: Research Press, 1972

Useful for understanding the research base for the facilitative interpersonal dimensions of the Carkhuff Model in education. Contains introductions to Flanders Interaction Analysis and Bloom's cognitive processes as well as empathy, congruence and regard. Concludes that teachers with high levels of interpersonal skills have students who achieve more.

Aspy, D.N. and Roebuck, F.N.
Kids Don't Learn from People They Don't Like
Amherst, Massachusetts: Human Resource Development Press, 1977.

Useful for understanding the research base for the Carkhuff Model in teaching. Studies the differential effects of training in Flanders, Bloom and Carkhuff skills. Hundreds of teachers were trained. The effects on thousands of learners were studied. Significant gains were achieved on the following indices: student absenteeism and tardiness; student discipline and school crises; student learning skills and cognitive growth. Concludes that the Carkhuff model is the preferred teacher training model.

Berenson, B.G.
Belly-to-Belly and Back-to-Back: The Militant Humanism of Robert R. Carkhuff
Amherst, Massachusetts: Human Resource Development Press, 1975.

Useful for an understanding of the human assumptions underlying the human and educational resource development models of Carkhuff. Presents a collection of prose and poetry by Carkhuff. Concludes by challenging us to die growing.

Berenson, B.G. and Carkhuff, R.R.
The Sources of Gain in Counseling and Psychotherapy
New York: Holt, Rinehart and Winston, 1967.

Useful for an in-depth view of the different orientations to helping. Integrates the research of diverse approaches to helping. Concludes with a model of core conditions around which the different preferred modes of treatment make their own unique contributions to helpee benefits.

Berenson, B.G. and Mitchell, K.M.
Confrontation: For Better or Worse
Amherst, Massachusetts: Human Resource Development Press, 1974.

Useful for an in-depth view of confrontation and immediacy as well as the core interpersonal dimensions. Presents extensive experimental manipulation of core interpersonal skills and confrontation and immediacy. Concludes that while confrontation is never necessary and never sufficient, in the hands of an effective helper, it may be efficient for moving the helpee toward constructive gain or change.

Carkhuff,R.R., Berenson, D.H. and Pierce RM.
The Skills of Teaching: Interpersonal Skills
Amherst, Mass.: Human Resource Development Press, 1977

Useful for pre-service and inservice teachers. Includes attending, responding, personalizing, and initiating modules with classroom applications.

Berenson, S.R.; Carkhuff, R.R.; Berenson,
D.H. and Pierce, R.M.
The Do's and Don'ts of Teaching
Amherst, Massachusetts: Human
Resource Development Press, 1977.

Useful for pre-service and in-service
teachers. Lays out the interpersonal
skills of teaching and their effect in
the most basic form. Concludes that
effective teachers apply skills that
facilitate their learners' involvement
in learning.

Carkhuff, R.R.
Helping and Human Relations.
Vol. 1. Selection and Training
Vol. 2. Practice and Research
New York: Holt, Rinehart and Winston,
1969.

Useful for understanding the research
base for interpersonal skills in
counseling and education.
Operationalizes the helping process
in great detail. Presents extensive
research evidence for systematic
selection, training and treatment
procedures. Concludes that teaching
is the preferred mode of treatment
for helping.

Carkhuff, R.R.
The Development of Human Resources:
Education, Psychology and Social Change
New York: Holt, Rinehart and Winston,
1971.

Useful for understanding applications of human resource
development (HRD) models.
Describes and presents research
evidence for numerous applications
in helping skills training in human,
educational and community resource
development. Concludes that
systematic planning for human
delivery systems can be effectively
translated into human benefits.

Carkhuff, R.R.
The Art of Helping III
Amherst, Massachusetts: Human
Resource Development Press, 3rd Edition,
1977

Useful for learning helping skills.
Includes attending, responding,
personalizing and initiating modules.
Concludes that helping is a way of
life.

Carkhuff, R.R. and Berenson, B.G.
Beyond Counseling and Therapy
New York: Holt, Rinehart and Winston,
2nd Edition, 1977.

Useful for understanding of the core
interpersonal conditions and their
implications and applications. Adds
many core dimensions and factors
them out as responsive and initiative
dimensions. Includes an analysis of
the client-centered, existential,
psychoanalytic, trait-and-factor and
behavioristic orientations to helping.
Concludes that only the trait-and-
factor and behavioristic positions
make unique contributions to human
benefits over and above the core
conditions.

Carkhuff, R.R. and Berenson, B.G.
Teaching As Treatment
Amherst, Massachusetts: Human
Resource Development Press, 1976.

Useful for understanding the
development of a human technology.
Operationalizes the helping process
as teaching. Offers research evidence
for living, learning and working skills
development and physical, emotional
and intellectual outcomes. Concludes
that learning-to-learn is the fun-
damental model for living, learning
and working.

Carkhuff, R.R.; Berenson, D.H. and
Berenson, S.R.
**The Skills of Teaching—
Lesson Planning Skills**
Amherst, Massachusetts: Human
Resource Development Press, in press,
1977.

Useful for learning skills needed to
prepare for delivering content.
Organizes lessons by reviewing,
overviewing, presenting, exercising
and summarizing. Breaks the
organization down into a tell-show-
do format. Concludes that content
must be delivered in programmatic
ways in order to maximize learning.

Carkhuff, R.R.; Devine, J.; Berenson, B.G.;
Griffin, A.H.; Angelone, R.; Keeling, T.;
Patch, W. and Steinberg, H.
Cry Twice!
Amherst, Massachusetts: Human
Resource Development Press, 1973.

Useful for understanding the
ingredients of institutional change.
Details the people, programs and
organizational variables needed to
transform an institution from a
custodial to a treatment orientation.
Concludes that institutional change
begins with people change.

Carkhuff, R.R and Pierce, R.M.
Teacher As Person
Washington, D.C.: National Education
Association, 1976.

Useful for teachers interested in
ameliorating the effects of sexism and
racism. Includes modules and applications of interpersonal skills in the
school. Concludes that behaviors
teachers practice influence learning
students accomplish.

Rogers, C.R.; Gendlin, E.T.; Kiesler, D.
and Truax, C.B.
**The Therapeutic Relationship and
Its Impact**
Madison, Wisconsin: University of
Wisconsin Press, 1967.

Useful for understanding the
transitional phases in developing
HRD models. Presents extensive
evidence on training lay and
professional helpers as well as different orientations to helping.
Concludes that the core interpersonal
dimensions of empathy, respect and
genuineness are critical to effective
helping.

Truax, C.B. and Carkhuff, R.R.
**Toward Effective Counseling
and Therapy**
Chicago, Illinois: Aldine, 1967.

Useful for understanding the
historical roots of the HRD models.
Presents extensive evidence on client-
centered counseling for schizophrenic
patients. Concludes that core interpersonal dimensions of empathy,
regard and congruence are critical to
effective helping.

Also by  *Human Resource Development Press*

Teaching as Treatment
by Robert Carkhuff and Bernard Berenson, 286 pp. $11.95
Teaching as the preferred mode of helping people with chapters on a teaching-helping model, learning outcomes, learning processes, teaching skills, a teaching as treatment delivery system and human values in a human technology.

Teacher as Person
National Education Association
by Robert Carkhuff and Richard Pierce, 61 pp., $5.95
An introductory manual for teaching the multi-cultural implications of interpersonal skills. Includes chapters on utilizing attending skills, responding skills, personalizing skills and initiating skills to combat racism and sexism in the classroom.

Helping Begins at Home
by Robert Carkhuff and Richard Pierce, 150 pp., $6.95
A skills manual for parents that operationalizes the parents' role in their children's growth and development. With chapters on facilitating physical growth, emotional growth and intellectual growth through skills acquisition.

The Art of Helping—Trainer's Guide
by Robert Carkhuff and Richard Pierce, 323 pp., $11.95
The teacher-trainer's guide to delivering life skills, with chapters on a developmental model of helping, teaching attending skills, teaching responding skills, teaching initiating skills and trainer instructions.

The Art of Developing a Career—Helper's Guide
by Ted Friel and Robert Carkhuff, 275 pp., $11.95
The teacher-trainer's guide to career skills development including sections on expanding career options, career decision-making skills, career short- and long-range planning and teaching methods.

Belly to Belly and Back to Back:
The Militant Humanism of Robert R. Carkhuff
by Bernard Berenson (Ed.), 102 pp., $9.95
A statement of the principles of a militant, humanistic philosophy upon which a human technology is being built.